World Economics /

Book Serie

Volume 4

On the use and misuse of theories and models in mainstream economics

Titles produced by the World Economics Association & College Publications

Piketty's *Capital in the Twenty-First Century*
Edward Fullbrook and Jamie Morgan, eds.

Volume 1
The Economics Curriculum: Towards a Radical reformulation
Maria Alejandra Maki and Jack Reardon, eds.

Volume 2
Finance as Warfare
Michael Hudson

Volume 3
Developing an economics for the post-crisis world
Steve Keen

Volume 4
On the use and misuse of theories and models in mainstream economics
Lars Pålsson Syll

The **World Economics Association (WEA)** was launched on May 16, 2011. Already over 13,000 economists and related scholars have joined. This phenomenal success has come about because the WEA fills a huge gap in the international community of economists – the absence of a professional organization which is truly international and pluralist.

The World Economics Association seeks to increase the relevance, breadth and depth of economic thought. Its key qualities are worldwide membership and governance, and inclusiveness with respect to: (a) the variety of theoretical perspectives; (b) the range of human activities and issues which fall within the broad domain of economics; and (c) the study of the world's diverse economies.

The Association's activities centre on the development, promotion and diffusion of economic research and knowledge and on illuminating their social character.

The WEA publishes 20+ books a year, three open-access journals (*Economic Thought, World Economic Review* and *Real-World Economics Review*), a bi-monthly newsletter, blogs, holds global online conferences, runs a textbook commentaries project and an eBook library.

www.worldeconomicassociation.org

On the use and misuse of theories and models in mainstream economics

Lars Pålsson Syll

© Lars Pålsson Syll, WEA and College Publications 2016.

All rights reserved.

ISBN 978-1-84890-184-1 print
ISBN 978-1-911156-19-2 eBook-PDF

Published by College Publications on behalf of the World Economics Association

http://www.worldeconomicsassociation.org
http://www.collegepublications.co.uk

Cover artwork: section from *Efflorescence*, Paul Klee, 1937, oil and pencil on cardboard. Phillips Collection

Printed by Lightning Source, Milton Keynes, UK

Contents

Introduction

Following the greatest economic depression since the 1930s, the grand old man of modern economic growth theory, Nobel laureate Robert Solow, on July 20, 2010, gave a prepared statement on "Building a Science of Economics for the Real World" for a hearing in the U. S. Congress. According to Solow modern macroeconomics has not only failed at solving present economic and financial problems, but is "bound" to fail. Building dynamically stochastic general equilibrium models (DSGE) on "assuming the economy populated by a representative agent" – consisting of "one single combination worker-owner-consumer-everything-else who plans ahead carefully and lives forever" – do not pass "the smell test: does this really make sense?" One cannot but concur in Solow's surmise that a thoughtful person "faced with the thought that economic policy was being pursued on this basis, might reasonably wonder what planet he or she is on."

We will get back to the "representative agent model" later. But although it is one of the main reasons for the deficiencies in modern (macro)economic theory, it is far from the only modeling assumption that does not pass the smell taste. In fact in this book it will be argued that modern orthodox (neoclassical) economic theory *in general* does not pass the smell test at all.

The recent economic crisis and the fact that orthodox economic theory has had next to nothing to contribute in understanding it, shows that neoclassical economics – in Lakatosian terms – is a degenerative research program in dire need of replacement.

Tradition has it that theories are carriers of knowledge about real world target systems and that models are of little consequence in this regard. It is no longer so. Especially not in economics (here, and elsewhere in the book, "economics" should be read as "orthodox, mainstream, neoclassical economics") where "the model is the message" has been the slogan for at least half a century. Today the models are the carriers of knowledge in the realm of "the queen of social sciences". The distinction formerly made within science theory between theories, as a collection of descriptive existential and relational statements about what is in the world, and models as simplified representations of a particular domain of reality, is definitely blurred in contemporary economics. Both theories and models are (partial) representations of certain properties considered important to emphasis for certain aims. In most contexts within a largely quantifiable science that insists on the exclusive use of methods of mathematical deductivist reasoning – as economics – "theory" and "model" are substitutable.

> On this general view of the nature of economic theory then, a 'theory' is not a collection of assertions about the behavior of the actual economy but rather an explicit set of instructions for building a parallel or analogue system – a mechanical, imitation economy. A 'good' model, from this point of view, will not be exactly more 'real' than a poor one, but will provide better imitations [Lucas 1981:272].

But economic theory has not been especially successful – not even by its own criteria of delivering explanations and understanding of real world economic systems.

> Modern economics is sick. Economics has increasingly become an intellectual game played for its own sake and not for its practical consequences for understanding the economic world. Economists have converted the subject into a sort of social mathematics in which analytical rigor is everything and practical relevance is nothing [Blaug 1997:3].

So how can it be this mathematical deductivist project of economic theory prevails?

> [P]robably the most compelling reason why the emphasis on mathematical deductive reasoning is retained, despite everything, is that it facilitates a second orientation that is conceptually separate. This is a concern with forecasting or *prediction* ... The possibility of successful prediction relies

on the occurrence of closed systems, those in which event regularities occur. And these, of course, are also precisely the required conditions for mathematical deductive reasoning to be practically useful, conditions therefore effectively presupposed by the (ubiquitous) reliance upon such methods [Bigo 2008:534].

Friedman (1953:15) claimed – rather oddly – that the descriptive realism of a theory has to be judged by its ability to yield "sufficiently accurate predictions." But as Sen (2008:627) notices, to check whether a prediction actually occurs, "there surely must be some idea of descriptive accuracy ... and this has to come before the concept of predictive accuracy can be entertained." Prediction depends on description, not the other way round.

One of the major problems of economics, even today, is to establish an empirical discipline that connects our theories and models to the actual world we live in. In that perspective I think it is necessary to replace both the theory and methodology of the predominant neoclassical paradigm. Giving up the neoclassical creed does not mean that we will have complete theoretical chaos.

The essence of neoclassical economic theory is its exclusive use of a deductivist Euclidean methodology. A methodology – which Arnsperger & Varoufakis [2006:12] calls the neoclassical meta-axioms of "methodological individualism, methodological instrumentalism and methodological equilibration" – that is more or less imposed as *constituting* economics, and, usually, without a smack of argument. Hopefully this book will manage to convey the need for an articulate feasible alternative – an alternative grounded on a relevant and realist open-systems ontology and a non-axiomatic methodology where social atomism and closures are treated as far from ubiquitous.

At best unhelpful, if not outright harmful, present day economic theory has come to way's end [cf. Syll 2011:145-48]. We need to shunt the train of economics onto a relevant and realist track. This could be done with the help of some under-labouring by critical realism and the methodological ideas presented in the works of the philosophers and economists such as for example Nancy Cartwright, John Maynard Keynes, Tony Lawson, Peter Lipton and Uskali Mäki.

But before dwelling on that theme, allow me to start by offering some comments on economics and the basic conditions for its feasibility from the perspective of methodology and science theory – in order that I can return later to the future of economics.

I will argue from a realist perspective for a science directed towards finding deep structural explanations and shed light on why standard economic analysis, founded on unrealistic and reductionist premises, is frequently found to have a rather limited applicability.

There is a tendency in mainstream economics to generalize its findings, as though the theoretical *model* applies to all societies at all times. I would argue that a critical realist perspective can work as a healthy antidote to over-generalized and a-historical economics.

One of the most important tasks of social sciences is to explain the events, processes, and structures that take place and act in society. In a time when scientific relativism (social constructivism, postmodernism, de-constructivism etc.) is expanding, it's important to guard against reducing science to a pure discursive level [cf. Pålsson Syll 2005]. We have to maintain the Enlightenment tradition of thinking of reality as principally independent of our views of it and of the main task of science as studying the structure of this reality. Perhaps the most important contribution a researcher can make is to reveal what this reality actually looks like. This is after all the object of science.

Science is made possible by the fact that there are structures that are durable and independent of our knowledge or beliefs about them. There exists a reality beyond our theories and concepts of it. It is this independent reality that is in some senses dealt with by our theories. Contrary to positivism, I cannot see that the main task of science is to detect event-regularities between observed facts. Rather, the task must be conceived as identifying the underlying structure and forces that produce the observed events.

Introduction

The problem with positivist social science is not that it gives the wrong answers, but rather that it does not, in a strict sense, give any answers at all. Its explanatory models presuppose that the social reality is "closed". Since social reality is fundamentally "open," models of that kind cannot explain what happens in such a universe.

In face of the kind of methodological individualism and rational choice theory that dominate positivist social science we have to admit that even if knowledge of the aspirations and intentions of individuals could be considered to be *necessary* prerequisites for providing explanations of social events, this knowledge is far from *sufficient*. Even the most elementary "rational" actions presuppose the existence of social forms that are irreducible to the intentions of individuals.

The overarching flaw with methodological individualism and rational choice theory, in their different guises, is basically that they reduce social explanations to purportedly individual characteristics. However, many of the characteristics and actions of the individual originate in and are only made possible through society and its relations. Even though society is not an individual following his own volition, and the individual is not an entity given outside of society, the actor and the structure have to be kept analytically distinct. They are tied together through the individual's reproduction and transformation of already given social structures.

It is here that I think that some social theorists falter. In economics, the economy is treated as a sphere that can be analyzed as if it were outside the community. What makes knowledge in social sciences possible is the fact that society consists of social structures and positions that influence the individuals, partly since they create the necessary prerequisites for the actions of individuals, but also because they predispose individuals to act in a certain way.

Even if we have to acknowledge that the world is mind-independent, this does not in any way reduce the epistemological fact that we can only know what the world is like from within our languages, theories, or discourses. But that the world is epistemologically *mediated* by theories does not mean that it is the *product* of them.

On the use and misuse of theories and models in economics

Our observations and theories are concept-*dependent* without therefore necessarily being concept-*determined*. There is a reality that exists independently of our knowledge and theories. Although we cannot comprehend it without using our concepts and theories, these are not the same as reality itself.

Social science is relational. It studies and uncovers the social structures in which individuals participate and position themselves. It is these relations that have sufficient continuity, autonomy, and causal power to endure in society and provide the real object of knowledge in social science. It is also only in their capacity as social relations and positions that individuals can be given power or resources – or the lack of them. To be a capital-owner or a slave is not an individual property, but can only come about when individuals are integral parts of certain social structures and positions. Just as a cheque presupposes a banking system and tribe-members presuppose a tribe – social relations and contexts cannot be reduced to individual phenomena.

The theories and models that economists construct describe imaginary worlds using a combination of formal sign systems such as mathematics and ordinary language. The descriptions made are extremely thin and to a large degree disconnected to the specific contexts of the targeted system than one (usually) wants to (partially) represent. This is not by chance. These closed formalistic-mathematical theories and models are constructed for the purpose of being able to deliver purportedly rigorous deductions that may somehow by be exportable to the target system. By analyzing a few causal factors in their "laboratories" they hope they can perform "thought experiments" and observe how these factors operate on their own and without impediments or confounders.

Unfortunately, this is not so. The reason for this is that economic causes never act in a socio-economic vacuum. Causes have to be set in a contextual structure to be able to operate. This structure has to take some form or other, but instead of incorporating structures that are true to the target system, the settings made in economic models are rather based on formalistic mathematical tractability. In the models they appear as unrealistic assumptions, usually playing a decisive role in getting the deductive machinery deliver "precise" and "rigorous" results. As noted by Frank Hahn

Introduction

[1994:246] – one of the icons of neoclassical mathematical economics – "the assumptions are there to enable certain results to emerge and not because they are to be taken descriptively." This, of course, makes exporting to real world target systems problematic, since these models – as part of a deductivist covering-law tradition in economics – are thought to deliver general and far-reaching conclusions that are externally valid. But how can we be sure the lessons learned in these theories and models have external validity, when based on highly specific unrealistic assumptions? As a rule, the more specific and concrete the structures, the less generalizable the results. Admitting that we *in principle* can move from (partial) falsehoods in theories and models to truth in real world target systems does not take us very far, unless a thorough explication of the relation between theory, model and the real world target system is made. If models *assume* representative actors, rational expectations, market clearing and equilibrium, and we *know* that real people and markets cannot be expected to obey these assumptions, the warrants for supposing that conclusions or hypothesis of causally relevant mechanisms or regularities can be bridged, are obviously non-justifiable. To have a deductive warrant for things happening in a closed model is no guarantee for them being preserved when applied to an open real world target system.

Economic theorists ought to do some ontological reflection and heed Keynes' [1936: 297] warnings on using models in economics:

> The object of our analysis is, not to provide a machine, or method of blind manipulation, which will furnish an infallible answer, but to provide ourselves with an organized and orderly method of thinking out particular problems; and, after we have reached a provisional conclusion by isolating the complicating factors one by one, we then have to go back on ourselves and allow, as well as we can, for the probable interactions of the factors amongst themselves. This is the nature of economic thinking. Any other way of applying our formal principles of thought (without which, however, we shall be lost in the wood) will lead us into error.

On the use and misuse of theories and models in economics

What is (wrong with) economic theory?

Most models in science are representations of something else. Models "stand for" or "depict" specific parts of a "target system" (usually the real world). A model that has neither surface nor deep resemblance to important characteristics of real economies ought to be treated with *prima facie* suspicion. How could we possibly learn about the real world if there are no parts or aspects of the model that have relevant and important counterparts in the real world target system? The burden of proof lays on the theoretical economists thinking they have contributed anything of scientific relevance without even hinting at any bridge enabling us to traverse from model to reality. All theories and models have to use sign vehicles to convey some kind of content that may be used for saying something of the target system. But purpose-built assumptions, like invariance, made solely to secure a way of reaching deductively validated results in mathematical models, are of little value if they cannot be validated outside of the model.

All empirical sciences use simplifying or unrealistic assumptions in their modeling activities. That is (no longer) the issue. Theories are difficult to directly confront with reality. Economists therefore build models of their theories. Those models are *representations* that are *directly* examined and manipulated to *indirectly* say something about the target systems.

The problem is however that the assumptions made in economic theories and models simply are unrealistic in the wrong way and for the wrong reasons.

There are economic methodologists and philosophers that argue for a less demanding view on modeling and theorizing in economics. And to some theoretical economists, as for example Robert Sugden, it is deemed quite enough to consider economics as a mere "conceptual activity" where "the model is not so much an abstraction from reality as a *parallel reality*" [2002:131]. By considering models as such *constructions*, Sugden distances the model from the intended target, for although "the model world is *simpler* than the real world, the one is not a *simplification* of the other" [2002:131]. The models only have to be *credible*, thereby enabling the economist to make inductive inferences to the target systems.

But what gives license to this leap of faith, this "inductive inference"? Within-model inferences in formal-axiomatic models are usually deductive, but that does not come with a warrant of reliability for inferring conclusions about specific target systems. Since all models in a strict sense are false (necessarily building in part on false assumptions) deductive validity cannot guarantee epistemic truth about the target system (cf. [Mäki 2011] on the relation between "truth bearer" in the model and "truth maker" in the real world target system). To argue otherwise would surely be an untenable overestimation of the epistemic reach of "surrogate models".

Being able to model a credible world, a world that somehow could be considered real or *similar* to the real world, is not the same as investigating the real world. Even though all theories are false, since they simplify, they may still possibly serve our pursuit of truth. But then they cannot be unrealistic or false in *any* way. The falsehood or unrealisticness has to be qualified (in terms of resemblance, relevance, etc.). At the very least, the minimalist demand on models in terms of credibility has to give away to a stronger epistemic demand of "*appropriate similarity and plausibility*" [Syll 2001:60]. One could of course also ask for a *sensitivity* or *robustness* analysis. But although Kuorikoski/Lehtinen [2009:130] considers "derivational robustness ... a way of seeing whether we can derive credible results from a set of incredible worlds", the credible world, even after having tested it for sensitivity and robustness, can still be a far way from reality – and unfortunately often in ways we know are important.

Robustness of claims in a model does not *per se* give a warrant for exporting the claims to real world target systems. The same can be seen in experimental economics and the problem of what Smith [1982:936] calls *parallelism*. Experimental economists attempt to get control over a large variety of variables, and to that aim they have to specify the experimental situation in a specific and narrow way. The more the experimentalist achieves control over the variables, the less the results they discover are applicable to the real world target systems. One would of course think it most likely that parallelism would hold for e. g. auctions, where we have a naturally demi-closed system in relative isolation and with a transparent and simple internal logic. As Alexandrova [2008:401] however shows, economic theory is unable to account even for this case, which the economists themselves consider to be a paradigm example of model application, the main reason being that "many more factors turned out to be relevant than was thought at first".

And even if "the economic method is very model oriented" and "the ideal of economic theory is to explain as much as possible with a as little as possible" [Torsvik 2006: 60], the simple fact of being in the laboratory or the economic theoretician's model does not necessarily cross any application domains. This (perhaps) sad conclusion reminds of Cartwright's [1999:37] view that if scientific laws "apply only in very special circumstances, then perhaps they are true just where we see them operating so successfully – in the artificial environment of our laboratories, our high-tech firms, or our hospitals".

Anyway, robust theorems are exceedingly rare or non-existent in economics. Explanation, understanding and prediction of real world phenomena, relations and mechanisms therefore cannot be grounded (solely) on robustness analysis. And as Cartwright [1989] forcefully has argued, some of the standard assumptions made in neoclassical economic theory – on rationality, information-handling and types of uncertainty – are not possible to make more realistic by "de-idealization" or "successive approximations" without altering the theory and its models fundamentally.

If we cannot show that the mechanisms or causes we isolate and handle in our models are stable – in the sense that what when we export them from are models to our target systems they do not change – then they only hold under *ceteris paribus* conditions and *a fortiori* are of limited value for our understanding, explanation and prediction of our real world target system. As Keynes [1973(1921):276-468] writes:

> The kind of fundamental assumption about the character of material laws, on which scientists appear commonly to act, seems to me to be [that] the system of the material universe

must consist of bodies ... such that each of them exercises its own separate, independent, and invariable effect, a change of the total state being compounded of a number of separate changes each of which is solely due to a separate portion of the preceding state ... Yet there might well be quite different laws for wholes of different degrees of complexity, and laws of connection between complexes which could not be stated in terms of laws connecting individual parts ... If different wholes were subject to different laws *qua* wholes and not simply on account of and in proportion to the differences of their parts, knowledge of a part could not lead, it would seem, even to presumptive or probable knowledge as to its association with other parts ... These considerations do not show us a way by which we can justify induction ... /427 No one supposes that a good induction can be arrived at merely by counting cases. The business of strengthening the argument chiefly consists in determining whether the alleged association is *stable*, when accompanying conditions are varied ... /468 In my judgment, the practical usefulness of those modes of inference ... on which the boasted knowledge of modern science depends, can only exist ... if the universe of phenomena does in fact present those peculiar characteristics of atomism and limited variety which appears more and more clearly as the ultimate result to which material science is tending.

Haavelmo [1944:28] basically says the same when discussing the stability preconditions for successful application of econometric methods in terms of autonomy:

> If we should make a series of speed tests with an automobile, driving on a flat, dry road, we might be able to establish a very accurate functional relationship between the pressure on the gas throttle ... and the corresponding maximum speed of the car ... But if a man did not know anything about automobiles, and he wanted to understand

how they work, we should not advise him to spend time and effort in measuring a relationship like that. Why? Because (1) such a relation leaves the whole inner mechanism of a car in complete mystery, and (2) such a relation might break down at any time, as soon as there is some disorder or change in any working part of the car ... We say that such a relation has very little *autonomy*, because its existence depends upon the simultaneous fulfillment of a great many other relations, some of which are of a transitory nature.

If the world around us is heterogeneous and organic, mechanisms and causes do not follow the general law of composition. The analogy of vector addition in mechanics simply breaks down in typical economics cases. The postulated stability just is not there since there are "interactive effects" between causes.

Uskali Mäki has repeatedly over the years argued for the necessity of "isolating by idealization," by which the theoretical economist can close the system (model) and "control for noise so as to isolate some important fact, dependency relation, causal factor or mechanism" [2009:31]. Sugden's "surrogate systems" view downplays the role of "sealing off" by *isolation* and rather emphasizes the *construction* part of modeling. The obvious ontological shortcoming of this epistemic approach is that "similarity" or "resemblance" *tout court* do not guarantee that the correspondence between model and target is interesting, relevant, revealing or somehow adequate in terms of mechanisms, causal powers, capacities, or tendencies. No matter how many convoluted refinements of general equilibrium concepts made in the model, if the model is not similar in the appropriate respects (such as structure, isomorphism, etc.), the surrogate system becomes a *substitute* system that does not bridge to the world but rather misses its target.

To give up the quest for truth and to merely study the internal logic of credible worlds is not compatible with scientific realism. To argue – as Kuorikoski & Lehtinen [2009:126] – that modeling can be conceived as "extended cognition" that may "legitimately change our beliefs about the world" may possibly be true, but is too modest a goal for science to go for. It is not even enough demanding inference from models to conclusions about the real world. One has to – as Mäki [2009:41] argues – "infer to conclusions about the world that are true or are likely to be true about the world … Justified model-to-world inference requires the model to be a credible surrogate system in being conceivable and perhaps plausible insofar as what it isolates – the mechanism – is concerned."

Modeling may – as argued by [Weisberg 2007:209] – be conceived of as a three stage enterprise. "In the first stage, a theorist constructs a model. In the second, she analyzes, refines, and further articulates the properties and dynamics of the model. Finally, in the third stage, she assesses the relationship between the model and the world if such an assessment is appropriate."

There are however philosophers and theoretical economists, like Gibbard & Varian [1978], who may be considered *outré* constructivist modelers, skipping the third stage and giving up all pretense of their *caricature* models and theories – built on a "deliberate distortion of reality" [671] and for which there is "no standard independent of the accuracy of the conclusions of the applied model for when its assumptions are sufficiently realistic" [671] – representing any *real* target systems. But if so, why should we invest time in studying purely hypothetical imaginary entities? If our theorizing does not consist in "forming explicit hypotheses about situations and testing them," how could it be that the economist "thinks the model will help to explain something about the world" [676]? What is it that caricature models can establish? As noted by, e.g., Rosenberg [1978:683], it is hard to come up with justifiable reasons to treat *fictionalism* a feasible modeling strategy in social science.

Weisberg [2007:224] says that even though "no assessment of the model-world relationship" is made, the insights gained from the analysis "may be useful in understanding real phenomena". That may be, but is – if viewed as an acceptable aspiration-level for scientific activity – too undemanding. And assessing the adequacy of a theory or model *solely* in terms of "the interests of the theorist" [Weisberg 2007:225] or "on purely aesthetic grounds" [Varian 1998: 241] does not seem to be a warranted scientific position. That would be lowering one's standards of fidelity beyond reasonable limits. Theories and models must be justified on *more* grounds than their intended scope or the fact that "most economic theorists admit that they do economics because it is fun" [Varian 1998:241]. Scientific theories and models must have ontological constraints and the most non-negotiable of these is – at least from a realist point of view – that they have to be coherent to the way the worlds is.

Even though we might say that models are devised "to account for stylized facts or data" [Knuutila 2009:75] and that "if conditions of the real world approximate sufficiently well the assumptions ... the derivations from these assumptions will be approximately correct [Simon 1963:230] – as Lawson [1997:208] aptly puts it, "a supposed 'stylised fact' is intended to express a partial regularity reformulated as a strict one, in the form of a law." I cannot but concur. Models as "stylized facts" or "stylized pictures" somehow "approximating" reality are rather unimpressive attempts at legitimizing using fictitious idealizations for reasons more to do with model tractability than with a genuine interest of understanding and explaining features of real economies. Many of the model-assumptions standardly made by neoclassical economics are *restrictive* rather than *harmless* and could *a fortiori* anyway not in any sensible meaning be considered approximations at all.

Knuuttila [2009:86] notices that most economic models fall short of representing real systems. I agree. Neoclassical economic theory employs very few principles, and among those used, bridge principals are as a rule missing. But instead of criticizing this (as I would) she rather apologetically concludes that "the connections between the models and the data, or what is known about economies more generally, are just looser than what is traditionally assumed" [2009:76]. To my ears this sounds like trying to turn failure into virtue. Why should we be concerned with economic models that are "purely hypothetical constructions" [2009:76]? Even if the constructionist approach should be able to accommodate the way we learn from models, it is of little avail to treat models as some kind "artefacts" or "heuristic devices" that produce claims, if they do not also connect to real world target systems.

Constructing "minimal economic models" may – even though they are without "world-linking conditions" [Grüne-Yanoff 2009:81] – affect our confidence in conjectures about the real world. And being able to explain relations between imaginary entities in "analogue" or "fictitious" models may increase our confidence in "inferential links to other bodies of knowledge" [Knuuttila 2009:77]. But this does not justify the conclusion that "correctly judging models to be credible does neither imply that they are true, nor that they resemble the world in certain ways, nor that they adhere to relevant natural laws" [Grüne-Yanoff 2009:95]. The final court of appeal for economic models is the real world, and as long as no convincing justification is put forward for how the confidence-enhancing takes place or the inferential bridging *de facto* is made, credible counterfactual worlds is little more than "hand waving" that give us rather little warrant for making inductive inferences from models to real world target systems. Inspection of the models shows that they have features that strongly influence the results obtained in them and that will not be shared by the real world target systems. Economics becomes exact but exceedingly narrow since "the very special assumptions do not fit very much of the contemporary economy around us" [Cartwright 1999:149]. Or as Krugman [2000:41] noted on an elaboration of the Mundell-Fleming macro model: "it is driven to an important extent by the details of the model, and can quite easily be undone. The result offers a tremendous clarification of the issues; it's not at all clear that it offers a comparable insight into what really happens."

If substantive questions about the real world are being posed, it is the formalistic-mathematical representations utilized to analyze them that have to match reality, not the other way around. "Economics is a science of thinking in terms of models joined to the art of choosing models which are relevant to the contemporary world. It is compelled to be this, because, unlike the natural science, the material to which it is applied is, in too many respects, not homogeneous through time" [Keynes 1971-89 vol XIV:296].

Taking lessons from models to the real world is demanding. To think that we are "invited to infer the likelihood of similar causes" [Sugden 2009:10] from the similarity of effects is overly optimistic. Abduction is not just inference to a *possible* explanation. To cut ice it has to be an inference to the *best* explanation. "Of course, there is always more than one possible explanation for any phenomenon ... so we cannot infer something simply because it is a possible explanation. It must somehow be the best of competing explanations" [Lipton 2004:56].

Sugden's rather – at least among present-day economists – typical view is far from sufficing. Economists also have to ask questions of how the models and theories contribute to explaining and understanding the real world target system.

Paradigmatic examples

To get a more particularized and precise picture of what neoclassical economic theory is today, it is indispensible to complement the perhaps rather "top-down" approach hitherto used with a more "bottom-up" approach. To that end I will below present – with emphasis on the chosen model-building strategy - three paradigmatic examples to exemplify and diagnose neoclassical economic theory as practiced nowadays.

Lucas understanding of business cycles

Economic theory is nowadays, as we have seen, in the story-telling business whereby economic theorists create make-believe analogue models of the target system – usually conceived as the real economic system. This modeling activity is considered useful and essential. Since fully-fledged experiments on a societal scale as a rule are prohibitively expensive, ethically indefensible or unmanageable, economic theorists have to substitute experimenting with something else. To understand and explain relations between different entities in the real economy the predominant strategy is to build models and make things happen in these "analogue-economy models" rather than engineering things happening in real economies.

In business cycles theory these models are according to Lucas constructed with the purpose of showing that changes in the supply of money "have the capacity to induce depressions or booms" [1988:3] not just in these models, but also in real economies. To do so economists are supposed to imagine subjecting their models to some kind of "operational experiment" and "a variety of reactions". "In general, I believe that one who claims to understand the principles of flight can reasonably be expected to be able to make a flying machine, and that understanding business cycles means the ability to make them too, in roughly the same sense" [1981:8]. To Lucas models are the *laboratories* of economic theories, and after having made a simulacrum-depression Lucas hopes we find it "convincing on its own terms – that what I said would happen in the [model] as a result of my manipulation would in fact happen" [1988:4]. The clarity with which the effects are seen is considered "the key advantage of operating in simplified, fictional worlds" [1988:5].

On the flipside lies the fact that "we are not really interested in understanding and preventing depressions in hypothetical [models]. We are interested in our own, vastly more complicated society" [1988:5]. But how do we bridge the gulf between model and "target system"? According to Lucas we have to be willing to "argue by analogy from what we know about one situation to what we would like to know about another, quite different situation" [1988:5]. Progress lies in the pursuit of the ambition to "tell better and better stories" [1988:5], simply because that is what economists do.

> "We are storytellers, operating much of the time in worlds of make believe. We do not find that the realm of imagination and ideas is an alternative to, or retreat from, practical reality. On the contrary, it is the only way we have found to think seriously about reality. In a way, there is nothing more to this method than maintaining the conviction ... that imagination and ideas matter ... there is no practical alternative" [1988:6].

Lucas has applied this mode of theorizing by constructing "make-believe economic systems" to the age-old question of what causes and constitutes business cycles. According to Lucas the standard for what that means is that one "exhibits understanding of business cycles by constructing a *model* in the most literal sense: a fully articulated artificial economy, which behaves through time so as to imitate closely the time series behavior of actual economies" [1981:219].

To Lucas business cycles is an inherently systemic phenomenon basically characterized by conditional co-variations of different time series. The vision

18

is "the possibility of a unified explanation of business cycles, grounded in the general laws governing market economies, rather than in political or institutional characteristics specific to particular countries or periods" [1981:218]. To be able to sustain this view and adopt his "equilibrium approach" he has to define the object of study in a very constrained way [cf. Vercelli 1991:11-23]. Lucas asserts, e.g., that if one wants to get numerical answers "one needs an explicit, equilibrium account of the business cycles" [1981:222]. But his arguments for why it necessarily has to be an *equilibrium* is not very convincing, but rather confirms Hausman's view [2001:320] that faced with the problem of explaining adjustments to changes, economists "have become complacent about this inadequacy — they have become willing prisoners of the limitations of their theories." The main restriction is that Lucas only deals with purportedly invariable regularities "common to all decentralized market economies" [1981:218]. Adopting this definition he can treat business cycles as all alike "with respect to the qualitative behavior of the co-movements among series" [1981:218]. As noted by Hoover [1988:187]:

> Lucas's point is not that all estimated macroeconomic relations are necessarily not invariant. It is rather that, in order to obtain an invariant relation, one must derive the functional form to be estimated from the underlying choices of individual agents. Lucas supposes that this means that one must derive aggregate relations from individual optimization problems taking only tastes and technology as given.

Postulating invariance paves the way for treating various economic entities as stationary stochastic processes (a standard assumption in most modern probabilistic econometric approaches) and the possible application of "economic equilibrium theory." The result is that Lucas business cycle is a rather watered-down version of what is usually connoted when speaking of business cycles.

Based on the postulates of "self-interest" and "market clearing" Lucas has repeatedly stated that a pure equilibrium method is a necessary intelligibility condition and that disequilibria are somehow "arbitrary" and "unintelligible"

[1981:225]. Although this might (arguably) be requirements put on models, these requirements are irrelevant and totally without justification vis-à-vis the real world target system. Why should involuntary unemployment, for example, be considered an unintelligible disequilibrium concept? Given the lack of success of these models when empirically applied (cf. Ball [1999], Estrella & Fuhrer [2002] and Seidman [2005]), what is unintelligible, is rather to pursue in this reinterpretation of the ups and downs in business cycles and labour markets as equilibria. To Keynes involuntary unemployment is not equatable to actors on the labour market becoming irrational non-optimizers. It is basically a reduction in the range of working-options open to workers, regardless of any volitional optimality choices made on their part. Involuntary unemployment is excess supply of labour. That unemployed in Lucas business cycles models only can be conceived of as having chosen leisure over work is not a substantive argument about real world unemployment.

> The point at issue [is] whether the concept of involuntary unemployment actually delineates circumstances of economic importance ... If the worker's reservation wage is higher than all offer wages, then he is unemployed. This is his preference given his options. For the new classicals, the unemployed have placed and lost a bet. It is sad perhaps, but optimal [Hoover 1988:59].

Sometimes workers are not employed. That is a real phenomenon and not a "theoretical construct ... the task of modern theoretical economics to 'explain'" [Lucas 1981:243].

All economic theories have to somehow deal with the daunting question of uncertainty and risk. It is "absolutely crucial for understanding business cycles" [1981:223]. To be able to practice economics at all, "we need some way ... of understanding which decision problem agents are solving" [1981:223]. Lucas – in search of a "technical model-building principle" [1981:1] – adapts the rational expectations view, according to which agents' subjective probabilities are identified "with observed frequencies of the events to be forecast" are coincident with "true" probabilities. This hypothesis [1981:224]:

will *most* likely be useful in situations in which the probabilities of interest concern a fairly well defined recurrent event, situations of 'risk' [where] behavior may be explainable in terms of economic theory ... In cases of uncertainty, economic reasoning will be of no value ... Insofar as business cycles can be viewed as repeated instances of essentially similar events, it will be reasonable to treat agents as reacting to cyclical changes as 'risk', or to assume their expectations are *rational*, that they have fairly stable arrangements for collecting and processing information, and that they utilize this information in forecasting the future in a stable way, free of systemic and easily correctable biases.

To me this seems much like putting the cart before the horse. Instead of adapting the model to the object – which from both ontological and epistemological considerations seem the natural thing to do – Lucas proceeds in the opposite way and chooses to define his object and construct a model solely to suit own methodological and theoretical preferences. All those – interesting and important - features of business cycles that have anything to do with model-theoretical openness, and *a fortiori* not possible to squeeze into the closure of the model, are excluded. One might rightly ask what is left of that we in a common sense meaning refer to as business cycles. Einstein's dictum – "everything should be made as simple as possible but not simpler" falls to mind. Lucas – and neoclassical economics at large – does not heed the implied apt warning.

The development of macro-econometrics has according to Lucas supplied economists with "detailed, quantitatively accurate replicas of the actual economy" thereby enabling us to treat policy recommendations "as though they had been experimentally tested" [1981:220]. But if the goal of theory is to be able to make accurate forecasts this "ability of a model to imitate actual behavior" does not give much leverage. What is required is "invariance of the structure of the model under policy variations". Parametric invariance in an economic model cannot be taken for granted, "but it seems reasonable to hope that neither tastes nor technology vary systematically" [1981:220].

On the use and misuse of theories and models in economics

The model should enable us to posit contrafactual questions about what would happen if some variable was to change in a specific way. Hence the assumption of structural invariance, that purportedly enables the theoretical economist to do just that. But does it? Lucas appeals to "reasonable hope", a rather weak justification for a modeler to apply such a far-reaching assumption. To warrant it one would expect an argumentation that this assumption – whether we conceive of it as part of a strategy of "isolation", "idealization" or "successive approximation" – really establishes a useful relation that we can export or bridge to the target system, the "actual economy." That argumentation is neither in Lucas, nor – to my knowledge – in the succeeding neoclassical refinements of his "necessarily artificial, abstract, patently 'unreal'" analogue economies [1981:271]. At most we get what Lucas himself calls "inappropriately maligned" casual empiricism in the form of "the method of keeping one's eyes open." That is far from sufficient to warrant any credibility in a model pretending to explain the complex and difficult recurrent phenomena we call business cycles. To provide an empirical "illustration" or a "story" to back up your model do not suffice. There are simply too many competing illustrations and stories that could be exhibited or told.

As Lucas has to admit – complaining about the less than ideal contact between theoretical economics and econometrics – even though the "stories" are (purportedly) getting better and better, "the necessary interaction between theory and fact tends not to take place" [1981:11].

The basic assumption of this "precise and rigorous" model therefore cannot be considered anything else than an unsubstantiated conjecture as long as it is not supported by evidence from outside the theory or model. To my knowledge no in any way decisive empirical evidence have been presented. This is the more tantalizing since Lucas himself stresses that the presumption "seems a sound one to me, but it must be defended on empirical, not logical grounds" [1981:12].

And applying a "Lucas critique" on Lucas' own model, it is obvious that it too fails. Changing "policy rules" cannot just be presumed not to influence investment and consumption behavior and a fortiori technology, thereby contradicting the invariance assumption. Technology and tastes cannot live

22

up to the status of an economy's deep and structurally stable Holy Grail. They too are part and parcel of an ever-changing and open economy. Lucas' hope of being able to model the economy as "a FORTRAN program" and "gain some confidence that the component parts of the program are in some sense reliable prior to running it" [1981:288] therefore seems – from an ontological point of view – totally misdirected. The failure in the attempt to anchor the analysis in the alleged stable deep parameters "tastes" and "technology" shows that if you neglect ontological considerations pertaining to the target system, ultimately reality kicks back when at last questions of bridging and exportation of model exercises are laid on the table. No matter how precise and rigorous the analysis is, and no matter how hard one tries to cast the argument in "modern mathematical form" [1981:7] they do not push science forwards one millimeter if they do not stand the acid test of relevance to the target. No matter how clear, precise, rigorous or certain the inferences delivered inside these models are, they do not *per se* say anything about external validity.

Formalistic deductive "Glasperlenspiel" can be very impressive and seductive. But in the realm of science it ought to be considered of little or no value to simply make claims about the model and lose sight of the other part of the model-target dyad.

Representative-agent models

Without export certificates models and theories should be considered unsold. Unfortunately this understanding has not informed modern economics, as can be seen by the profuse use of so called representative-agent models.

A common feature of economics is to use simple general equilibrium models where representative actors are supposed to have complete knowledge, zero transaction costs and complete markets.

In these models, the actors are all identical. For someone holding the view that "economics is based on a superficial view of individual and social behavior" and thinks "it is exactly this superficiality that gives economics much of the power that it has: its ability to predict human behavior without knowing very much about the makeup and lives of the people whose behavior we are trying to understand " [Lucas1986:241], it is natural to consider it "helpful" to elaborate his theory with the help of a "representative agent" and build an "abstract model economy" with "N identical individuals" [1981:68] operating in "two markets" that are "structurally identical" and have "no communication between them" [1981:72] within each trading period.

This has far-reaching analytical implications. Situations characterized by asymmetrical information – situations most of us consider to be innumerable – cannot arise in such models. If the aim is to build a macro-analysis from micro-foundations in this manner, the relevance of the procedure is highly questionable. Solow [2010:2] – in the congressional hearing referred to in the introduction – even considers the claims made by protagonists of rational agent models "generally phony".

One obvious critique is that representative-agent models do not incorporate distributional effects – effects that often play a decisive role in macroeconomic contexts. Investigations into the operations of markets and institutions usually find that there are overwhelming problems of coordination. These are difficult, not to say impossible, to analyze with the kind of Robinson Crusoe models that, e. g., real business cycle theorists employ and which exclude precisely those differences between groups of actors that are the driving force in many non-neoclassical analysis.

The choices of different individuals have to be shown to be coordinated and consistent. This is obviously difficult if the economic models don't give room for heterogeneous individuals (this lack of understanding the importance of heterogeneity is perhaps especially problematic for the modeling of real business cycles in dynamic stochastic general equilibrium models, cf. [Hansen & Heckman 1996]). Representative-agent models are certainly more manageable, however, from a realist point of view, they are also less relevant and have a lower explanatory potential.

Both the "Lucas critique" and Keynes' critique of econometrics [cf. Syll 2007b:20-25] argued that it was inadmissible to project history on the future. Consequently an economic policy cannot presuppose that what has worked before, will continue to do so in the future. That macroeconom(etr)ic models could get hold of correlations between different "variables" was not enough. If they could not get at the causal structure that generated the data, they were not really "identified". Lucas himself drew the conclusion that the problem with unstable relations was to construct models with clear microfoundations where forward-looking optimizing individuals and robust, deep, behavioural parameters are seen to be stable even to changes in economic policies.

To found macroeconomics on the actions of separate individuals, is an example of methodological reductionism, implying that macro-phenomena can be uniquely inferred from micro-phenomena. Among science-theoreticians this is a contested standpoint. Even though macro-phenomena somehow *presuppose* micro-phenomena, it is far from certain that they can be *reduced to* or *deduced from* them.

In microeconomics we know that aggregation really presupposes homothetic an identical preferences, something that almost never exist in real economies. The results given by these assumptions are therefore not robust and do not capture the underlying mechanisms at work in any real economy. And as if this was not enough, there are obvious problems also with the kind of microeconomic equilibrium that one tries to reduce macroeconomics to. Decisions of consumption and production are described as choices made by a single agent. But then, who sets the prices on the market? And how do we justify the assumption of universal consistency between the choices?

Kevin Hoover [2010b:27-28] has argued that the representative-agent models also introduce an improper idealization:

> The representative agent is held to follow the rule of perfect competition, price-taking, which is justified on the idealizing assumptions that $n = > \infty$; yet the representative agent is itself an idealization in which $n = > 1$. The representative agent is – inconsistently – simultaneously the whole market and small relative to market. The problem can be summed by the question: with whom does the representative agent trade?

On the use and misuse of theories and models in economics

Models that are critically based on particular and odd assumptions – and are neither robust nor congruent to real world economies – are of questionable value.

And is it really possible to describe and analyze all the deliberations and choices made by individuals in an economy? Does not the choice of an individual presuppose knowledge and expectations about choices of other individuals? It probably does, and this presumably helps to explain why representative-agent models have become so popular in modern macroeconomic theory. They help to make the analysis more tractable.

One could justifiably argue that one might just as well accept that it is not possible to coherently reduce macro to micro, and accordingly that it is perhaps necessary to forswear microfoundations and the use of rational-agent models all together. Microeconomic reasoning has to build on macroeconomic presuppositions. Real individuals do not base their choices on operational general equilibrium models, but rather use simpler models. If macroeconomics needs *micro*foundations it is equally necessary that microeconomics needs *macro*foundations.

The philosopher John Searle [1995] has asserted that their might exist something he calls "collective intentionality". Given the existence of the latter, one might be able to explain to economists the enigmatic behaviour of for example people who vote in political elections. The aggregate outcome is decided by the collective intentions of the citizens, such as "it is your duty as citizen to vote". To deduce this outcome from a representative actor's behaviour without taking account of such intentions or institutions, is simply not possible.

The microeconomist Alan Kirman [1992] has maintained that the use of representative-agent models is unwarranted and leads to conclusions that are usually both misleading and false. It is a fiction basically used by some macroeconomists to justify the use of equilibrium analysis and a kind of pseudo-microfoundations. Microeconomists are well aware that the conditions necessary to make aggregation to representative actors possible, are not met in actual economies. As economic models become increasingly complex, their use also becomes less credible.

What is (wrong with) economic theory?

Even if economies naturally presuppose individuals, it does not follow that we can *infer* or *explain* macroeconomic phenomena solely from knowledge of these individuals. Macroeconomics is to a large extent *emergent* and cannot be reduced to a simple summation of micro-phenomena. Moreover, even these microfoundations aren't immutable. Lucas and the new classical economists' deep parameters – "tastes" and "technology" – are not really the bedrock of constancy that they believe (pretend) them to be.

Now I do not think there is an unbridgeable gulf between micro and macro. We just have to accept that micro-macro relations are so complex and manifold, that the former cannot somehow be *derived* from the latter.

For Marshall [1951:171] economic theory was "an engine for the discovery of concrete truth". But where Marshall tried to describe the behaviour of a typical business with the concept "representative firm", his modern heirs don't at all try to describe how firms interplay with other firms in an economy. The economy is rather described "as if" consisting of one single giant firm – either by inflating the optimization problem of the individual to the scale of a whole economy, or by assuming that it's possible to aggregate different individuals' actions by a simple summation, since every type of actor is identical. But do not we just have to face that it is difficult to describe interaction and cooperation when there is essentially only *one* actor?

To economists for whom macroeconomic analysis is largely geared to trying to understand macroeconomic externalities and coordination failures, representative-agent models are particularly ill-suited. In spite of this, these models are frequently used, giving rise to a neglect of the aggregation-problem. This highlights the danger of letting the model, rather than the method, become the message.

Econometrics

Economists often hold the view that criticisms of econometrics are the conclusions of sadly misinformed and misguided people who dislike and do not understand much of it. This is really a gross misapprehension. To be careful and cautious is not the same as to dislike. And as any perusal of the mathematical-statistical and philosophical works of people like for example

On the use and misuse of theories and models in economics

Nancy Cartwright, Chris Chatfield, Kevin Hoover, Hugo Keuzenkamp, John Maynard Keynes, Tony Lawson or Arios Spanos would show, the critique is put forward by respected authorities. I would argue, against "common knowledge", that they do not misunderstand the crucial issues at stake in the development of econometrics. Quite the contrary. They know them all too well – and are not satisfied with the validity and philosophical underpinning of the assumptions made for applying its methods.

Let me try to do justice to the critical arguments on the logic of probabilistic induction and shortly elaborate – mostly from a philosophy of science vantage point – on some insights critical realism gives us on econometrics and its methodological foundations.

The methodological difference between an empiricist and a deductivist approach, that we have already commented on, can also clearly be seen in econometrics. The ordinary deductivist "textbook approach" views the modeling process as foremost an estimation problem, since one (at least implicitly) assumes that the model provided by economic theory is a well-specified and "true" model. The more empiricist, general-to-specific-methodology (often identified as "the LSE approach") on the other hand views models as theoretically and empirically adequate representations (approximations) of a data generating process (DGP). Diagnostics tests (mostly some variant of the F-test) are used to ensure that the models are "true" – or at least "congruent" – representations of the DGP (cf. Chao [2002]). The modeling process is here more seen as a specification problem where poor diagnostics results may indicate a possible misspecification requiring re-specification of the model. The objective is standardly to identify models that are structurally stable and valid across a large time-space horizon. The DGP is not seen as something we already know, but rather something we discover in the process of modeling it. Considerable effort is put into testing to what extent the models are structurally stable and generalizable over space and time.

Although I have sympathy for this approach in general, there are still some unsolved "problematics" with its epistemological and ontological presuppositions [cf. Lawson 1989, Keuzenkamp 2000 and Pratten 2005]. There is, e. g., an implicit assumption that the DGP fundamentally has an invariant property and that models that are structurally unstable just have not been able to get hold of that invariance. But, as already Keynes maintained, one cannot just presuppose or take for granted that kind of invariance. It has to be argued and justified. Grounds have to be given for viewing reality as satisfying conditions of model-closure. It is as if the lack of closure that shows up in the form of structurally unstable models somehow could be solved by searching for more autonomous and invariable "atomic uniformity". But if reality is "congruent" to this analytical prerequisite has to be argued for, and not simply taken for granted.

Even granted that closures come in degrees, we should not compromise on ontology. Some methods simply introduce improper closures, closures that make the disjuncture between models and real world target systems inappropriately large. "Garbage in, garbage out."

Underlying the search for these immutable "fundamentals" lays the implicit view of the world as consisting of material entities with their own separate and invariable effects. These entities are thought of as being able to be treated as separate and additive causes, thereby making it possible to infer complex interaction from knowledge of individual constituents with limited independent variety. But, again, if this is a justified analytical procedure cannot be answered without confronting it with the nature of the objects the models are supposed to describe, explain or predict. Keynes himself thought it generally inappropriate to apply the "atomic hypothesis" to such an open and "organic entity" as the real world. As far as I can see these are still appropriate strictures all econometric approaches have to face. Grounds for believing otherwise have to be provided by the econometricians.

Trygve Haavelmo, the "father" of modern probabilistic econometrics, wrote that he and other econometricians could not "build a complete bridge between our models and reality" by logical operations alone, but finally had to make "a non-logical jump" [1943:15]. A part of that jump consisted in that econometricians "like to believe ... that the various a priori possible sequences would somehow cluster around some typical time shapes, which if we knew them, could be used for prediction" [1943:16]. But since we do not know the true distribution, one has to look for the mechanisms (processes) that "might rule the data" and that hopefully persist so that predictions may be made. Of all possible hypotheses on different time sequences – "samples" in Haavelmo's somewhat idiosyncratic vocabulary – most had to be ruled out a priori "by economic theory", although "one shall always remain in doubt as to the possibility of some ... outside hypothesis being the true one" [1943:18].

The limits of econometric forecasting has – as noted by Qin (2013:110) – been critically pointed out many times:

> There have been over four decades of econometric research on business cycles ... The formalization has undeniably improved the scientific strength of business cycle measures ...

> But the significance of the formalization becomes more difficult to identify when it is assessed from the applied perspective, especially when the success rate in ex-ante forecasts of recessions is used as a key criterion. The fact that the onset of the 2008 financial-crisis-triggered recession was predicted by only a few 'Wise Owls' ... while missed by regular forecasters armed with various models serves us as the latest warning that the efficiency of the formalization might be far from optimal. Remarkably, not only has the performance of time-series data-driven econometric models been off the track this time, so has that of the whole bunch of theory-rich macro dynamic models developed in the wake of the rational expectations movement, which derived its fame mainly from exploiting the forecast failures of the macro-econometric models of the mid-1970s recession.

Trygve Haavelmo – with the completion (in 1958) of the twenty-fifth volume of Econometrica – assessed the role of econometrics in the advancement of economics, and although mainly positive of the "repair work" and "clearing-up work" done, Haavelmo [1958:353] also found some grounds for despair:

> We have found certain general principles which would seem to make good sense. Essentially, these principles are based

on the reasonable idea that, if an economic model is in fact "correct" or "true," we can say something a priori about the way in which the data emerging from it must behave. We can say something, a priori, about whether it is theoretically possible to estimate the parameters involved. And we can decide, a priori, what the proper estimation procedure should be ... But the concrete results of these efforts have often been a seemingly lower degree of accuracy of the would-be economic laws (i.e., larger residuals), or coefficients that seem a priori less reasonable than those obtained by using cruder or clearly inconsistent methods.

There is the possibility that the more stringent methods we have been striving to develop have actually opened our eyes to recognize a plain fact: viz., that the "laws" of economics are not very accurate in the sense of a close fit, and that we have been living in a dream-world of large but somewhat superficial or spurious correlations.

And as the quote below shows, even Ragnar Frisch [Louçã (2007:206)] shared some of Haavelmo's – and Keynes's – doubts on the applicability of econometrics:

I have personally always been skeptical of the possibility of making macroeconomic predictions about the development that will follow on the basis of given initial conditions ... I have believed that the analytical work will give higher yields – now and in the near future – if they become applied in macroeconomic decision models where the line of thought is the following: If this or that policy is made, and these conditions are met in the period under consideration, probably a tendency to go in this or that direction is created.

To Haavelmo and his modern followers, econometrics is not really in the truth business. The explanations we can give of economic relations and structures based on econometric models are "not hidden truths to be discovered" but rather our own "artificial inventions". Models are consequently perceived not as true representations of DGP, but rather instrumentally conceived "as if"-constructs. Their "intrinsic closure" is realized by searching for parameters showing "a great degree of invariance" or relative autonomy and the "extrinsic closure" by hoping that the "practically decisive" explanatory variables are relatively few, so that one may proceed "as if ... natural limitations of the number of relevant factors exist" [Haavelmo 1944:29].

Just like later Lucas, Haavelmo seems to believe that persistence and autonomy can only be found at the level of the individual, since individual agents are seen as the ultimate determinants of the variables in the economic system.

But why the "logically conceivable" really should turn out to be the case is difficult to see. At least if we are not satisfied by sheer hope. As we have already noted Keynes reacted against using unargued for and unjustified assumptions of complex structures in an open system being reducible to those of individuals. In real economies it is unlikely that we find many "autonomous" relations and events. And one could of course, with Keynes and from a critical realist point of view, also raise the objection that to invoke a probabilistic approach to econometrics presupposes, e.g., that we have to be able to describe the world in terms of risk rather than genuine uncertainty.

And that is exactly what Haavelmo [1944:48] does: "To make this a rational problem of statistical inference we have to start out by an axiom, postulating that every set of observable variables has associated with it one particular 'true', but unknown, probability law."

But to use this "trick of our own" and just assign "a certain probability law to a system of observable variables", however, cannot – just as little as hoping – build a firm bridge between model and reality. Treating phenomena *as if* they essentially were stochastic processes is not the same as showing that they essentially *are* stochastic processes. Rigour and elegance in the analysis does not make up for the gap between reality and model. It is the distribution of the phenomena in itself and not its estimation that ought to be at the centre of the stage. A crucial ingredient to any economic theory that wants to use probabilistic models should be a convincing argument for the view that "there can be no harm in considering economic variables as stochastic variables" [Haavelmo 1943:13]. In most cases no such arguments are given.

Hendry acknowledges that there is a difference between the actual DGP and the models we use trying to adequately capture the essentials of that real world DGP. He also criticizes forecasting procedures based on the assumption that the DGP is constant. That kind of closure just is not there in the world as we know it. When "we don't know what we don't know," it is preposterous to build models assuming an ergodic DGP. It's like assuming that there does exist a "correct" model and that this is the actual DGP whose constant parameters we just have to estimate. That is hard to take seriously. If such invariant parameters and concomitant regularities exist, has to be assessed *ex post* and not be assumed as an axiom in model-construction. This has to be an empirical question. The proof of the pudding is in the eating.

Like Haavelmo, Hendry assumes that what we observe are random variables which we can treat *as if* produced in accordance with a complex joint probability distribution. If we are performing a fully-controlled experiment or a Monte Carlo simulation this is of course true, since we control the characteristics of the DGP ourselves. But in the time series we work with in applied econometrics, is that really a tenable position? Can we really come to identify, know and access the DGP outside experiment-like situations? Hendry would insist that even if the answer to these questions is no, constructing useful models and theories of econometrics is still possible. From an instrumentalist point of view you may have good reasons for wanting to design a useful model that bridges the gap between "theory and empirical evidence" [Hendry 1995:359]. You may even persist in the hope that there exist "invariant features of reality" since otherwise "neither theories nor econometric models would be of much practical value" [Hendry 2000:474]. But it's a slippery slope. Hendry and other econometricians sometimes have a tendency to conflate the DGP as a hypothesis and as an actual reality. This placing model on a par with reality is an example of what Marx called reification and is from a methodological and scientific-theoretic point of view an untenable equivocation. But where some methodologists of econometrics, like Hugo Keuzenkamp [2000:154], want to get rid of the ambiguity by dropping the idea of the DGP as an actual process and treat it solely as an invention of our mind, one could rather argue that we have to drop the idea that we in our models ever can be sure that we have got hold of the Holy Grail of econometrics – the DGP.

Of course you are entitled – like Haavelmo and his modern probabilistic followers – to express a hope "at a metaphysical level" that there are invariant features of reality to uncover and that also show up at the empirical level of observations as some kind of regularities.

But is it a *justifiable* hope? I have serious doubts. The kind of regularities you may hope to find in society is not to be found in the domain of surface phenomena, but rather at the level of causal mechanisms, powers and capacities. Persistence and generality has to be looked out for at an underlying deep level. Most econometricians do not want to visit that playground. They are content with setting up theoretical models that give us correlations and eventually "mimic" existing causal properties. The focus is on measurable data, and one even goes so far as defining science as "a public approach to the measurement and analysis of observable phenomena" [Hendry 1997:167]. Econometrics is basically made for *modeling* the DGP, and not to account for unobservable aspects of the real world target system (DGP).

We have to accept that reality has no "correct" representation in an economic or econometric model. There is no such thing as a "true" model that can capture an open, complex and contextual system in a set of equations with parameters stable over space and time, and exhibiting invariant regularities. To just "believe", "hope" or "assume" that such a model *possibly* could exist, is not enough. It has to be justified in relation to the ontological conditions of social reality. And as Toulmin [2003:34] so neatly puts it:

> In order for a suggestion to be a 'possibility' in any context … it must 'have what it takes' in order to be entitled to genuine consideration *in that context*. To say, in any field, 'Such-and-such is a possible answer to our question', is to say that, bearing in mind the nature of the problem

concerned, such-and-such an answer deserves to be considered. This much of the meaning of the term 'possible' is field-invariant. The criteria of possibility, on the other hand, are field-dependent, like the criteria of impossibility or goodness. The things we must point to in showing that something is possible will depend entirely on whether we are concerned with a problem in pure mathematics, a problem of team-selection, a problem in aesthetics, or what; and features which make something a possibility from one standpoint will be totally irrelevant from another.

In contrast to those who want to give up on (fallible, transient and transformable) "truth" as a relation between theory and reality and content themselves with "truth" as a relation between a model and a probability distribution, I think it is better to really scrutinize if this latter attitude is feasible. To just say "all models are wrong ... some, however, are useful" [Keuzenkamp 2000:116] is to defeatist. That is to confuse social engineering with science. To abandon the quest for truth and replace it with sheer positivism would indeed be a sad fate of econometrics. It is more rewarding to stick to truth as a regulatory ideal and keep on searching for theories and models that in relevant and adequate ways express those parts of reality we want to describe and explain.

Econometrics may be an informative tool for research. But if its practitioners do not investigate and make an effort of providing a justification for the credibility of the assumptions on which they erect their building, it will not fulfill its tasks. There is a gap between its aspirations and its accomplishments, and without more supportive evidence to substantiate its claims, critics will continue to consider its ultimate argument as a mixture of rather unhelpful metaphors and metaphysics. Maintaining that economics is a science in the "true knowledge" business, I remain a skeptic of the pretences and aspirations of econometrics. So far, I cannot really see that it has yielded very much in terms of relevant, interesting economic knowledge.

The marginal return on its ever higher technical sophistication in no way makes up for the lack of serious under-labouring of its deeper philosophical and methodological foundations that already Keynes complained about. The rather one-sided emphasis of usefulness and its concomitant instrumentalist justification cannot hide that neither Haavelmo [cf. 1944:10] nor Hendry [cf. 2000:276] give supportive evidence for their considering it "fruitful to believe" in the possibility of treating unique economic data as the observable results of random drawings from an imaginary sampling of an imaginary population. After having analyzed some of its ontological and epistemological foundations, I cannot but conclude that econometrics on the whole has not delivered "truth". And I doubt if it has ever been the intention of its main protagonists.

Our admiration for technical virtuosity should not blind us to the fact that we have to have a more cautious attitude towards probabilistic inference of causality in economic contexts. Science should help us penetrate to "the true process of causation lying behind current events" and disclose "the causal forces behind the apparent facts" [Keynes 1971-89 vol XVII:427]. We *should* look out for causal relations, but econometrics can never be more than a starting point in that endeavour, since econometric (statistical) explanations are not explanations in terms of mechanisms, powers, capacities or causes [cf. Sayer 2000:22]. Firmly stuck in an empiricist tradition, econometrics is only concerned with the *measurable* aspects of reality. But there is always the possibility that there are other variables – of vital importance and although perhaps unobservable and non-additive not necessarily epistemologically inaccessible – that were not considered for the model. Those who *were* can hence never be *guaranteed* to be more than potential causes, and not real causes. As science-philosopher Mario Bunge [1979:53] once stated – "the reduction of causation to regular association ... amounts to mistaking causation for one of its tests."

A rigorous application of econometric methods in economics presupposes that the phenomena of our real world economies are ruled by stable causal relations between variables. Contrary to allegations of both Hoover [2002:156] and Granger [2004:105] I would say that a perusal of the leading econom(etr)ic journals shows that most econometricians still concentrate on fixed parameter models and that parameter-values estimated in specific spatio-temporal contexts are *presupposed* to be exportable to totally different contexts. To warrant this assumption one, however, has to convincingly establish that the targeted acting causes are stable and invariant so that they maintain their parametric status after the bridging. The endemic lack of predictive success of the econometric project indicates that this hope of finding fixed parameters is a hope for which there really is no other ground than hope itself.

This is a more fundamental and radical problem than the celebrated "Lucas critique" have suggested. This is not the question if deep parameters, absent on the macro-level, exist in "tastes" and "technology" on the micro-level. It goes deeper. Real world social systems are not governed by stable causal mechanisms or capacities. It is the criticism that Keynes [1951(1926): 232-33] first launched against econometrics and inferential statistics already in the 1920s:

> The atomic hypothesis which has worked so splendidly in Physics breaks down in Psychics. We are faced at every turn with the problems of Organic Unity, of Discreteness, of Discontinuity – the whole is not equal to the sum of the parts, comparisons of quantity fails us, small changes produce large effects, the assumptions of a uniform and homogeneous continuum are not satisfied. Thus the results of Mathematical Psychics turn out to be derivative, not fundamental, indexes, not measurements, first approximations at the best; and fallible indexes, dubious approximations at that, with much doubt added as to what, if anything, they are indexes or approximations of.

The kinds of laws and relations that econom(etr)ics has established, are laws and relations about entities in models that presuppose causal mechanisms being atomistic and additive (for an argumentation that this is also the case for experimental economics, cf. Siakantaris [2000:270]). When causal mechanisms operate in real world social target systems they only do it in ever-changing and unstable combinations where whole is more than a mechanical sum of parts. If economic regularities obtain they do it (as a rule) only because we engineered them for that purpose. Outside man-made "nomological machines" they are rare, or even non-existant. Unfortunately that also makes most of the achievements of econometrics – as most of contemporary endeavours of economic theoretical modeling – rather useless.

Why neoclassical economic theory is a dead end

The failures of mainstream macroeconomics are largely attributable to its use of deductivist theory and method. Its foundations are not as strong as Lucas and other neoclassical economists assume them to be. There's a huge gap between the purported ideal of building economics from the behaviour of individual actors and the fact that what one accomplishes has very little to do with the behaviour of real individuals. As Toulmin [2003:236] notes:

> If we ask about the validity, necessity, rigour or impossibility of arguments or conclusions, we must ask these questions within the limits of a given field, and avoid, as it were, condemning an ape for not being a man or a pig for not being a porcupine.

A realist and relevant economic theory has to do better. Even though there may be no royal road to success, I would contend neoclassical economics has definitely come to the end of the road.

Let me just give some hints of the kind of ontological and methodological building stones that are missing in neoclassical economics and that a viable alternative economic theory would have to work with.

Relevance, realism and the search for deep causal explanations

Instead of taking for granted that we are in possession of the one "correct" model, we have to have a more humble attitude. We know certain things and to know more we dig. We don't content ourselves with surface appearances and correlations between observable variables. We dig deep. Correlations between observables are clues and form the starting points in our search for deeper causal structures in economy and society. But they aren't invariant parameters *à la* "tastes" and "technology" in Lucas analysis of business cycles. As a famous philosopher once put it – "all that is solid melts into air". That goes for the alleged "deep parameters" too.

Economics can't be a "Euclidean" science. It reduces it to a logical axiomatic system in applied mathematics, with little bearing on real economies. As Keynes stated, we should use a more "Babylonian" approach and aim for less universal theories and accept that there will always be binding spatio-temporal restrictions to the validity of our theories. The real economy is – to use the words of Cartwright [1999] – no "nomological machine", but rather a "dappled" world.

As Wesley Salmon [1971:34] famously noted, one can *deduce* that a male person who takes birth-control pills will not get pregnant, but that surely does not *explain* why that person does not get pregnant. Economics should definitely be in the explanation business, and deductions, though not useless, is less helpful than citing relevant causes.

Paul Samuelson [1964:737] once wrote that to describe "how" was to explain, and that "economists as scientists shouldn't waste their time with unfruitful questions of "why?" To pose questions regarding underlying causes was considered metaphysical." As a critical realist I would rather say that a social science that doesn't pose "why-questions" can hardly count as a science at all.

Explanation and prediction are not the same. To explain something is to uncover the generative mechanisms behind an event, while prediction only concerns actual events and does not have anything to say about the underlying causes of the events in question. The barometer may be used for predicting today's weather changes. But these predictions are not explanatory, since they say nothing of the underlying causes.

Every social phenomenon is determined by a host of both necessary and contingent relations. It is also for this reason that we can never confidently predict them. As Maxine Singer [1997:39] has put it: "Because of the things we don't know that we don't know, the future is largely unpredictable."

On the use and misuse of theories and models in economics

If we want the knowledge we produce to have practical relevance, our knowledge-aspirations and methods have to adapt to our object of study. In social sciences – such as economics – we will never reach *complete* explanations. Instead we have to aim for *satisfactory* and *adequate* explanations.

As is well known, there is no unequivocal criterion for what should be considered a *satisfactory* explanation. All explanations (with the possible exception of those in mathematics and logic) are fragmentary and incomplete; self-evident relations and conditions are often left out so that one can concentrate on the nodal points. Explanations must, however, be real in the sense that they are "congruent" to reality and are capable of being used.

The *relevance* of an explanation can be judged only by reference to a given *aspect* of a problem. An explanation is then relevant if, for example, it can point out the generative mechanisms that rule a phenomenon or if it can illuminate the aspect one is concerned with. To be relevant from the explanatory viewpoint, the adduced theory has to provide a good basis for believing that the phenomenon to be explained really does or did take place. One has to be able to say: "That's right! That explains it. Now I understand why it happened."

While deductivist approaches try to develop a general *a priori* criterion for evaluation of scientific explanations, it would be better to realize that all we can expect to establish are *adequate* explanations, which it is not possible to disconnect from the specific, contingent circumstances that are always incident to what is to be explained.

Here I think that neoclassical economists go wrong in that they – at least implicitly – think their general models and theories are applicable to all kinds of societies and economies. But the insistence that all known economies have had to deal with scarcity in some form or other does not take us very far. I think we have to be more modest and acknowledge that our models and theories are time-space relative.

What is (wrong with) economic theory?

Besides being an aspect of the situation in which the event takes place, an explanatory factor ought also to be causally *effective* – that is, one has to consider whether the event would have taken place even if the factor did not exist. And it also has to be causally *deep*. If event e would have happened without factor f, then this factor is not deep enough. Triggering factors, for instance, often do not have this depth. And by contrasting different factors with each other we may find that some are irrelevant (without causal depth).

Without the requirement of depth, explanations most often do not have practical significance. This requirement leads us to the nodal point against which we have to take measures to obtain changes. If we, e. g., search for and find fundamental structural causes for unemployment, we can hopefully also take effective measures to remedy it.

Relevant scientific theories do more than just describe (purported) event-regularities. They also analyze and describe the mechanisms, structures, and processes that exist. They try to establish what relations exist between these different phenomena and the systematic forces that operate within the different realms of reality.

Explanations are important within science, since the choice between different theories hinges in large part on their explanatory powers. The most reasonable explanation for one theory's having greater explanatory power than others is that the mechanisms, causal forces, structures, and processes it talks of, really do exist.

When studying the relation between different factors, a neoclassical economist is usually prepared to admit the existence of a reciprocal interdependence between them. One is seldom prepared, on the other hand, to investigate whether this interdependence might follow from the existence of an underlying causal structure. This is really strange. The actual configurations of a river, for instance, depend – of course – on many factors. But one cannot escape the fact that it flows downhill and that this fundamental fact influences and regulates the other causal factors. Not to come to grips with the underlying causal power that the direction of the current constitutes can only be misleading and confusing.

41

On the use and misuse of theories and models in economics

All explanations of a phenomenon have preconditions that limit the number of alternative explanations. These preconditions significantly influence the ability of the different potential explanations to really explain anything. If we have a system where underlying structural factors control the functional relations between the parts of the system, a satisfactory explanation can never disregard this precondition. Explanations that take the micro-parts as their point of departure may well *describe* how and through which mechanisms something takes place, but without the macro-structure we cannot *explain* why it happens.

But could one not just say that different explanations – such as individual (micro) and structural (macro) – are different, without a need to grade them as better or worse? I think not. That would be too relativistic. For although we are dealing with two different kinds of explanations that answer totally different questions, I would say that the structural most often answers the more relevant questions. In social sciences we often search for explanations because we want to be able to avoid or change certain outcomes. Giving individualistic explanations does not make this possible, since they only state sufficient but not necessary conditions. Without knowing the latter we cannot prevent or avoid these undesirable social phenomena.

All kinds of explanations in empirical sciences have a pragmatic dimension. We cannot just say that one type is *false* and another is *true*. Explanations have a function to fulfill, and some are *better* and others *worse* at this. Even if individual explanations can show the existence of a pattern, the pattern as such does not constitute an explanation. We want to be able to explain the pattern *per se*, and for that we usually require a structural explanation. By studying statistics of the labor market, e. g., we may establish the fact that everyone who is at the disposal of the labor market does not have a job. We might even notice a pattern, that people in rural areas, old people, and women are often jobless. But we cannot explain with these data why this is a fact, and that it may even be that a certain amount of unemployment is a functional requisite for the market economy. The individualistic frame of explanation gives a false picture of what kind of causal relations are at hand, and *a fortiori* a false picture of what needs to be done to enable a change. For that, a structural explanation is required.

What is (wrong with) economic theory?

Taking complexity seriously

With increasing complexity comes a greater probability of systemic instability. Real economies are complex systems and they have to be analyzed with an eye to instability. Macroeconomics has to be founded on analyses of the behaviour of agents in disequilibrium. Stability considerations have to be made. Otherwise we are shadow-boxing. Just as increasing returns to scale, dynamic instability can no longer be ruled out just because it doesn't fit some preferred theoretical preconceptions or models. In moving equilibrium systems, the interesting things usually take place in-between, in the transitional phases.

A fallacy often made in neoclassical economics is the (implicit) assumption made, that the structure of the real system of which the model is supposed to be a (partial) representation of, is invariant. Structural changes, breaks, regime-switches and innovations are continually taking place and we cannot simply *assume* that the system is dynamically stable. It has to be justified and not just treated as "infinitely improbable".

With increasing complexity comes a greater probability of systemic instability. Real economies are complex systems and they have to be analyzed with an eye to instability. Macroeconomics has to be founded on analysis of behaviour of agents in disequilibrium. Stability considerations have to be made. Just as increasing returns to scale, dynamic instability can no longer be ruled out just because they do not fit some preferred theoretical preconceptions or models. Even though not sufficient in itself, sensibility analysis ought to be self-evident, since eventual equilibria without robustness are uninteresting coincidences in dynamically open systems. In continually moving equilibrium systems the interesting things take place in between, in the transitional phases.

The methodological implications of the awareness of these considerations are far-reaching. If the plausibility of analyzing the economy as a structurally stable system (partly) hinges on its degree of complexity, it is of cause of the outmost importance to use models and theories that are open to and able to reflect an ontologically complex economic system. Simply assuming structural stability without justification is unacceptable. It has to be convincingly argued that the real counterparts of our macroeconomic models and theories are in line with these assumptions. (At least if the aim of our scientific endeavours is more than predictive, also aspiring to explain the deeper mechanisms at work in the economy and having instruments to affect it.)

Rational expectations are used in new classical economics to analyze macroeconomic equilibria, and it does not really bother to really found it in actors' dynamic behaviour out-of-equilibrium. Lucas and other neoclassical economists just *assume* that the distribution of the possibilities of economic actors coincide with the distribution holding for the "real" data generating process. This implies the well-known description of actors as not committing systematic errors when predicting the future.

This kind of model presupposes – if it is to be applicable – that the stochastic economic processes are stationary. This in its turn means that the equilibrium is permanent and that the future is perfectly predictable. This kind of *ergodicity* is impossible to reconcile with history, irreversible time and actors learning by doing. How do you justify such a far-reaching assumption? Is it a self-evident axiom, a reasonable assumption describing real actors, empirically corroborated, an as-if assumption in the spirit of Friedmanian instrumentalism, or is it the only hypothesis of expectations formation that happens to be compatible with neoclassical axiomatic deductivist general equilibrium theory? I would take my bet on the last. The problem with this is that it is rather unenlightening from a realist viewpoint. What has to be argued is that actors that realize *ex post* that they have misjudged the situation and formed inadequate expectations, do learn from this and swiftly adapt their expectations so to instantly move towards a new (possibly permanent) equilibrium.

All *ad hoc* arguments for this view cannot do away with the obvious fact that once you allow for instability you also have to accept a certain degree of indeterminacy and the non-existence of event regularities. This is the only tenable way out of the model-conundrums that the hypothesis of rational expectations gets us into. If reality is to a large extent indeterminate, uncertain and instable, our model-assumptions have to reflect these ontological facts. There are regularities in the economy, but they are typically contextual, conditional and partial.

If we follow that path we, of course, have to give up the Euclidean hope of analyzing the economy as an axiomatic, deductively closed system. This is necessary. It is better to admit there are "things we don't know we don't know" and that therefore the future is uncertain in ways we don't know. Some economic factors are inherently unpredictable (as e. g. stock-market prices, foreign exchange rates etc.) and give rise to structural breaks, shifts and non-linearities and genuinely unanticipated events that disrupts any eventual equilibrium.

When the relation between map and reality is poor, we have to redraw the map. An economic model is only relevant to the economy if it somehow *resembles* it. Real economies are evolving over time and are intermittently subject to large and unanticipated shocks. They are non-stationary and over time they sometimes show great changes in all the moments of the distribution of its constituent variables.

Models based on the hypothesis of rational expectations are, to say the least, far from ideal representations of macroeconomic behaviour in such systems. If economists want to say something relevant of real economies and not only of "thought-of-economies" they have to develop other models and methods.

The need for methodological pluralism and abduction

Criticizing neoclassical economics is no license for a post-modern and social constructivist attitude of "anything goes". Far from it. There *are* limits to feasible methods and we *do* have criteria for choosing between them. As a critical realist, I'm acutely aware of the danger of sliding down the slippery slope of relativism. On the other hand, however, I think there's need for a large amount of open-mindedness when it comes to the choice of relevant methods [cf. Danermark et al. 2002:150-176]. As long as those choices reflect an argued and justified position vis-a-vis ontology we have to admit that different contexts may call for more than one method. Contrary to the beliefs of deductivist-axiomatic theorists – one size doesn't fit all.

On the use and misuse of theories and models in economics

Keynes [1936:297] maintained that "the object of our analysis is not to provide a machine, or method of blind manipulation, which will furnish an infallible answer." Strictly deductive argumentation is possible only in logic. "In … science, and in conduct, most of the arguments, upon which we habitually base our rational beliefs, are admitted to be inconclusive in a greater or less degree" [Keynes 1973(1921):3]. In economics you can't "convict your opponent of error" but only "convince him of it". Hence, the aim of economic reasoning can only be to "persuade a rational interlocutor" [Keynes 1971-89 vol XIII :470]. Economics is an *argumentative* science. Since you cannot really prove things, you have to argue and justify. And if one does use deductive arguments, one has to be aware of the limits of their validity and justify their use.

If this is the case, what kind of inferences should we aim for in economics? Arguably the most promising method is abduction – or *inference to the best explanation* as it is also called.

In abduction one infers "from the fact that a certain hypothesis would explain the evidence, to the truth of that hypothesis" [Harman 1965:89]. Or more schematically:

e is a collection of evidence
H would, if true, explain e
No other hypothesis can *explain* e as well as H does
– – – –
Therefore, H is (probably) true

In contradistinction to deduction and induction, it is neither logically necessary, nor an empirical generalization. It's rather reminiscent of Sherlock Holmes. Different frames of interpretation are tentatively deliberated, the problem is re-contextualized and with a little help from creativity and imagination, new connections and meanings are discovered, helping to solve the puzzle or explain the event or process. We don't know for sure that the new connections and meanings constitute true knowledge, but it's possible that they constitute better or deeper knowledge.

The scientific method should preferably be both *ampliative* – increase our knowledge – and also increase our *epistemic warrant* in the results it gives us. The best balance between these goals is given by abduction.

That the scientific method should extend our knowledge is a self-evident starting-point for a scientific realist. But it is not always easy to combine ampliation and epistemic warrant. What is it that gives warrant to one hypothesis rather than others when we go beyond our sensory impressions? A purely deductive method would ensure us that conclusions were as probative as the premises on which they build. But deduction is totally unampliative. Its output is in its truth-transmitting input. If we are to use content-increasing methods we therefore have to accept that they can't be of a deductive caliber. Our data never guarantees that only *one* hypothesis is valid. But on the other hand it does not follow that they possess *the same degree* of validity. All cats are not necessarily grey. If a standpoint is tenable cannot be decided solely on formal-logic considerations but has to take into account consideration of what the world is and how it is structured. That a method isn't the best in all possible worlds doesn't preclude it being the best in the world in which we happen to live. To hold the view that abduction is not an inference "can be upheld only if one entertains the implausible views that to infer is to deduce and that to infer is to have 'an automatic warrant' for the inference" [Psillos 2002:619].

What we infer with ampliative methods will always be more or less defeasible. In contrast to the either/or of Kierkegaard and deductivism, the inferences of an ampliative method can always be changed, modified or rejected as a result of more and new information or by having conducted better analysis.

The problem of induction is that its ampliation is narrow and builds on going from "some" instances to "all" via generalization. This "more of the same" method enhances our knowledge in a purely *horizontal* manner. No new entities, relations or structures emerge. In that regard, induction signifies a minimal ampliation of knowledge, based on an underlying assumption of the world as ruled by event-regularities. Its short-comings are obvious. What we gain in epistemic warrant we lose in strength of the ampliation. It is too restrictive to give us hypotheses or explanations of the causes behind observed phenomena.

In science, the hypothetic-deductive method makes possible a forceful ampliation through confirmation of posited hypothesis and opens up for using unobservable causes. As the Duhem-Quine problem exemplifies, it, however, does not help us in discriminating which of the assumptions or hypothesis that is wrong when the theory cannot be confirmed. If both hypotheses A and B may explain X, the hypothetic-deductive method doesn't give us any means to discriminate between them. What we gain in ampliation, we lose in epistemic warrant. The hypothetic-deductive method simply is too permitting, since it doesn't enable us to discriminate between different hypotheses that are compatible with the evidence. A method that can't rank hypotheses such as "contemporary Swedish unemployment is a result of Swedish workers being lazy" or "contemporary unemployment is a result of globalization, technological development and economic policy" simply isn't an adequate method.

Abduction, on the other hand, can rank competing hypotheses and tackles the Duhem-Quine problem, since it urges us to look beyond the properties and implications of single hypotheses and also judges and ranks their explanatory power. Abduction is both a logic of justification and a logic of discovery.

The trade-off between ampliation and epistemic warrant results from a kind of risk present in all ampliation, and the more risk we are willing to take the less epistemic warrant we have to live with. We get to know more, but are less sure of that which we know. If we want to have a larger degree of confidence in our knowledge we are usually forced to forgo new knowledge and its accompanying risks.

Then, having argued for abduction as striking the best balance between ampliation and epistemic warrant, what does a good abduction look like? A natural demand for a critical realist to posit is that it should establish a causal relation between explanandum and explanans. To say that H is the best explanation of X is simultaneously to say that of the hypothesis we are comparing, the causal story H paints is in best concordance with our background knowledge. The *contrastive* character of explanation [cf. Garfinkel 1981] is thereby emphasized since it is not possible to decide which explanation – out of many potential explanations – is the best, without taking account of relevant background knowledge.

There are, of course, other criteria that are mentioned when one tries to describe explanatory merit: consilience, depth, simplicity, precision. But even if these criteria often are desirable, they are not self-evident or even decisive for our evaluation of potential explanations. To a large extent they are pragmatic virtues and domain-specific in character.

If explanatory power in the shape of simplicity, unification, coherence, etc., has to do with truth is a matter you have to argue for. They *may* be criteria for theory-choice, but they *need* not be. These criteria chiefly express the more or less idiosyncratic preferences of different scientists. *Ceteris paribus* it is as a rule preferable to have a more unified, simpler or coherent theory. This you can defend from purely thought- and cognition-economic or esthetic considerations. But you cannot *a priori* maintain that they have to be better, more probable or truer than their rivals.

Probability and evidential weight

Almost a hundred years after John Maynard Keynes wrote his seminal *A Treatise on Probability* (1921), it is still very difficult to find statistics textbooks that seriously try to incorporate his far-reaching and incisive analysis of induction and evidential weight.

The standard view in statistics – and the axiomatic probability theory underlying it – is to a large extent based on the rather simplistic idea that "more is better." But as Keynes argues – "more of the same" is not what is important when making inductive inferences. It's rather a question of "more but different."

Variation, not replication, is at the core of induction. Finding that $p(x|y) = p(x|y \ \& \ w)$ doesn't make w "irrelevant." Knowing that the probability is unchanged when w is present gives $p(x|y \ \& \ w)$ another evidential weight ("weight of argument"). Running 10 replicative experiments do not make you as "sure" of your inductions as when running 10,000 varied experiments - even if the probability values happen to be the same.

According to Keynes we live in a world permeated by unmeasurable uncertainty – not quantifiable stochastic risk – which often forces us to make decisions based on anything but "rational expectations." Keynes rather thinks that we base our expectations on the confidence or "weight" we put on different events and alternatives. To Keynes expectations are a question of weighing probabilities by "degrees of belief," beliefs that often have preciously little to do with the kind of stochastic probabilistic calculations made by the rational agents as modeled by "modern" social sciences. And often we "simply do not know."

Science according to Keynes should help us penetrate to "the true process of causation lying behind current events" and disclose "the causal forces behind the apparent facts." Models can never be more than a starting point in that endeavour. He further argued that it was inadmissible to project history on the future. Consequently we cannot presuppose that what has worked before, will continue to do so in the future. That statistical models can get hold of correlations between different "variables" is not enough. If they cannot get at the causal structure that generated the data, they are not really "identified."

How strange that writers of statistics textbooks as a rule do not even touch upon these aspects of scientific methodology that seems to be so fundamental and important for anyone trying to understand how we learn and orient ourselves in an uncertain world. An educated guess on why this is a fact would be that Keynes concepts are not possible to squeeze into a single calculable numerical "probability." In the quest for quantities one puts a blind eye to qualities and looks the other way - but Keynes ideas keep creeping out from under the statistics carpet.

It's high time that statistics textbooks give Keynes his due.

What is (wrong with) economic theory?

Why it is better to be vaguely right than precisely wrong

When applying deductivist thinking to economics, the neoclassical economist usually sets up an "as if"-model based on a set of tight axiomatic assumptions from which consistent and precise inferences are made. The beauty of this procedure is, of course, that if the axiomatic premises are true, the conclusions necessarily follow. The snag is that if the models are to be relevant, we also have to argue that their precision and rigour still holds when they are applied to real-world situations. They often do not. When addressing real economies, the idealizations necessary for the deductivist machinery to work, simply do not hold.

So how should we evaluate the search for ever greater precision and the concomitant arsenal of mathematical and formalist models? To a large extent, the answer hinges on what we want our models to perform and how we basically understand the world.

For Keynes the world in which we live is inherently uncertain and quantifiable probabilities are the exception rather than the rule. To every statement about it is attached a "weight of argument" that makes it impossible to reduce our beliefs and expectations to a one-dimensional stochastic probability distribution. If "God does not play dice" as Einstein maintained, Keynes would add "nor do people". The world as we know it, has limited scope for certainty and perfect knowledge. Its intrinsic and almost unlimited complexity and the interrelatedness of its organic parts prevent the possibility of treating it as constituted by "legal atoms" with discretely distinct, separable and stable causal relations. Our knowledge accordingly has to be of a rather fallible kind.

To search for precision and rigour in such a world is self-defeating, at least if precision and rigour are supposed to assure external validity. The only way to defend such an endeavour is to take a blind eye to ontology and restrict oneself to prove things in closed model-worlds. Why we should care about these and not ask questions of relevance is hard to see. We have to at least justify our disregard for the gap between the nature of the real world and the theories and models of it.

On the use and misuse of theories and models in economics

Keynes [1971-89 vol XIV:296] once wrote that economics "is a science of thinking in terms of models joined to the art of choosing models which are relevant to the contemporary world." Now, if the real world is fuzzy, vague and indeterminate, then why should our models build upon a desire to describe it as precise and predictable? Even if there always has to be a trade-off between theory-internal validity and external validity, we have to ask ourselves if our models are relevant.

Models preferably ought to somehow reflect/express/partially represent/resemble reality. The answers are not self-evident, but at least one has to do some philosophical under-labouring to rest one's case. Too often that is wanting in modern economics, just as it was when Keynes in the 1930s complained about the econometricians' lack of justifications of the chosen models and methods.

"Human logic" has to supplant the classical, formal, logic of deductivism if we want to have anything of interest to say of the real world we inhabit. Logic is a marvellous tool in mathematics and axiomatic-deductivist systems, but a poor guide for action in real-world systems, in which concepts and entities are without clear boundaries and continually interact and overlap. In this world I would say we are better served with a methodology that takes into account that "the more we know the more we know we don't know".

The models and methods we choose to work with have to be in conjunction with the economy as it is situated and structured. Epistemology has to be founded on ontology. Deductivist closed-system theories, as neoclassical economic theory, could perhaps adequately represent an economy showing closed-system characteristics. But since the economy clearly has more in common with an open-system ontology, we ought to look out for other theories - theories who are rigorous and precise in the meaning that they can be deployed for enabling us to detect important causal mechanisms, capacities and tendencies pertaining to deep layers of the real world.

Rigour, coherence and consistency have to be defined relative to the entities for which they are supposed to apply. Too often they have been restricted to questions internal to the theory or model. Even if "the main role of deductive approaches is to guarantee consistency" [Moses & Knutsen 2007:282], clearly the nodal point has to concern external questions, such as how our theories and models relate to real-world structures and relations. Applicability rather than internal validity ought to be the arbiter of taste. There is no need to abolish economic theory altogether, but as Hicks [1984:215] noted, it needs to be carried on in a different way, "less abstract, more history-friendly, less technical, more concerned with real economic phenomena, less reductionist and more open to taking advantage of the contributions coming from other social and moral sciences."

Open systems, equilibrium, expectations and uncertainty

Expectations have to be treated in a context of real, *historical* time. Real individuals don't settle their accounts at the end of periods in general equilibrium *mechanical* time. Actors have to make decisions, plans and act in the absence of equilibrium. Most importantly, firms have to plan their investments in the light of a more or less uncertain future, where there may even not yet exist a market for their products and where the present economic outlook offers few guidelines. Output and employment – ruled by expectations – are largely indeterminate and the structure of the economy changes continually and in complex ways, making it extremely difficult to predict or model.

Since the alternative non-neoclassical framework is not restricted to *individuals*, there is an open possibility for investigating expectations-formation in different *groups*. Mores, conventions and norms differ between consumers, firms and governments. If they are strong, there might be a possibility to detect certain kinds of *demi-regularities* in their formation [cf. Lawson 1997:204-231].

It's also a fact that different groups have to tackle different *kinds* of uncertainty. For macroeconomics, the expectations of investors are as a rule the most important. Unfortunately these are strongly influenced by Keynes "animal spirits" which are extremely tricky to handle in analysis. Shocks and surprises repeatedly make it impossible to predict the shifting moods in spirit. No matter what the interest rates, animal spirits can suddenly shift and affect plans to invest. This increases the uncertainty in the sense of Keynes "weight of argument" view – confidence in our predictions fall.

On the use and misuse of theories and models in economics

This applies to both long-run predictions of the price of gold five years hence and to short-term predictions of exactly on which day and minute the asset markets turn and we need to cash in on our position.

This is also one of the main reasons why *money* plays such an important role in real economies. Money makes it possible to postpone investments and not commit ourselves until we are more confident in our expectations and predictions.

All this confirms the basic "problem" – the economy is an open system. This has to be reflected by our analytical aspirations. Anything else will only lead to continual frustration. Markets are not usually totally chaotic. However, when it comes to expectations and the future, Keynes *dictum* still stands – often "we simply don't know".

Individuals in neoclassical economics are usually assumed to be in a behavioural equilibrium and to have rational expectations. This assumption presupposes - if it's to be applicable – that the stochastic economic processes are stationary. This in turn means that the equilibrium is permanent and that the future is perfectly predictable. From a critical realist point of view, this is dubious. This kind of ergodicity is impossible to reconcile with history, irreversible time and actors learning by doing.

Once you allow for instability you also have to accept a certain degree of indeterminacy and the non-existence of event regularities. This is the only tenable way out of the model-conundrums that the hypothesis of rational expectations gets us into. If reality is indeterminate, uncertain and instable, our model-assumptions have to reflect these facts. There *are* regularities in the economy, but they are typically contextual, conditional and partial.

If we follow this path we have to give up the Euclidean hope of analyzing the economy as an axiomatic, deductively closed system. In my view this is essential.

Economic theory cannot just provide an economic model that *mimics* the economy. Theory is important but we can't start to question data when there is a discrepancy. This would presuppose an almost religious faith in the validity of the preferred theory. When the relation between map and reality is poor, we have to redraw the *map*.

When it comes to equilibrium a tenable non-neoclassical economic theory has to reject the mechanical time equilibrium used by mainstream macroeconomics since it is not possible to apply it to real world situations. Real-world phenomena such as creative destruction, new technologies and innovations are not really compatible with general equilibrium. Institutions, endogenous technology, increasing returns to scale, irreversible time, non-ergodicity and uncertainty are not – as has been repeatedly shown in history – easily incorporated within the neoclassical framework.

From an explanatory point of view, it is more feasible to use partial analysis and to try to give explanations in terms of what are deemed to be the most causally important variables in specific contexts, instead of trying to encapsulate everything in one single timeless interdependent general equilibrium model.

Epilogue

Let me round off this chapter with some remarks on where the great divide in economics is currently situated.

In the history of economics there have existed many different schools of economic thought. Some of them – especially neoclassical economics – we have touched upon here. They are usually contrasted in terms of the theories and models they use. However, the fundamental divide is really methodological. How we categorize these schools should basically refer to their underlying ontological and methodological preconceptions, and not, for example, to their policy implications, use of mathematics and the like.

Much analytical-philosophical efforts has lately been invested in untangling terminological a conceptual analysis of models and theories. I think this necessary and good. But it is certainly not sufficient. The use and misuse of different theoretical and modeling strategies also have to be evaluated and criticized.

On the use and misuse of theories and models in economics

To develop economics along critical realist lines it is necessary to give up the ill-founded use of closed representative-agent models, since these eliminate the basic problem of uncertainty and coordination between individual actors and groups, and make conventional behaviour totally unintelligible.

Henry Louis Mencken [1917] once wrote that "[t]here is always an easy solution to every human problem – neat, plausible and wrong". And neoclassical economics has indeed been wrong. Its main result, so far, has been to demonstrate the futility of trying to build a satisfactory bridge between formalistic-axiomatic deductivist models and real world target systems. Assuming, for example, perfect knowledge, instant market clearing and approximating aggregate behaviour with unrealistically heroic assumptions of representative actors, just will not do. The assumptions made, surreptitiously eliminate the very phenomena we want to study: uncertainty, disequilibrium, structural instability and problems of aggregation and coordination between different individuals and groups.

The punch line of this is that most of the problems that neoclassical economics is wrestling with, issues from its attempts at formalistic modeling *per se* of social phenomena. Reducing microeconomics to refinements of hyper-rational Bayesian deductivist models is not a viable way forward. It will only sentence to irrelevance the most interesting real world economic problems. And as someone has so wisely remarked, murder is unfortunately the only way to reduce biology to chemistry - reducing macroeconomics to Walrasian general equilibrium microeconomics basically means committing the same crime.

If scientific progress in economics – as Lucas and other latter days neoclassical economists seem to think – lies in our ability to tell "better and better stories" *without* considering the realm of imagination and ideas a retreat from real world target systems reality, one would of course think our economics journal being filled with articles supporting the stories with empirical evidence. However, the journals show a striking and embarrassing paucity of empirical studies that (try to) substantiate these theoretical claims. Equally amazing is how little one has to say about the relationship between the model and real world target systems. It is as though thinking explicit discussion, argumentation and justification on the subject not required. Economic theory is obviously navigating in dire straits.

Recent events in the financial markets have, as rightly noticed by Paul Krugman [2009], "pretty decisively refuted the idea that recessions are an optimal response to fluctuations in the rate of technological progress" and that "unemployment is a deliberate decision by workers to take time off". According to Krugman what went wrong was basically that "the economics profession went astray because economists, as a group, mistook beauty, clad in impressive-looking mathematics, for truth." This is certainly true as far as it goes. But it is not deep enough. Mathematics is just a means towards the goal – modeling the economy as a closed deductivist system.

If the ultimate criteria of success of a deductivist system is to what extent it predicts and coheres with (parts of) reality, modern neoclassical economics seems to be a hopeless misallocation of scientific resources. To focus scientific endeavours on proving things in models, is a gross misapprehension of what an economic theory ought to be about. Deductivist models and methods disconnected from reality are not relevant to predict, explain or understand real world economic target systems. These systems do not conform to the restricted closed-system structure the neoclassical modeling strategy presupposes. If we do not just want to accept that "in the social sciences what is treated as important is often that which happens to be accessible to measurable magnitudes" [Hayek 1974], critical realism can help make it possible to reorient our endeavours in more constructive directions (in macroeconomics, e. g. Jespersen [2009] is a valuable contribution) and build a relevant and realist economics that can provide advances in scientific understanding of real world economies.

In this book an attempt has been made to give an up-to-date coverage of recent research and debate on the highly contentious topic of the status and relevance of economic theory. It shows that what is wrong with economics is not that it employs models, but that it employs poor models. They are poor because they do not bridge to the real world target system in which we live. Economic theory today consists mainly in investigating economic models.

On the use and misuse of theories and models in economics

Neoclassical economics has since long given up on the real world and contents itself with proving things about thought up worlds. Empirical evidence only plays a minor role in economic theory (cf. Hausman [1997]), where models largely functions as a substitute for empirical evidence. Hopefully humbled by the manifest failure of its theoretical pretences, the one-sided, almost religious, insistence on mathematical deductivist modeling as the only scientific activity worthy of pursuing in economics will give way to methodological pluralism based on ontological considerations rather than formalistic tractability.

If not, we will have to keep on wondering – with Robert Solow and other thoughtful persons – what planet the economic theoretician is on.

Capturing causality in economics and the limits of statistical inference

A few years ago, Armin Falk and James Heckman published an acclaimed article in the journal *Science*. The authors – both renowned economists – argued that both field experiments and laboratory experiments are basically facing the same problems in terms of generalizability and external validity – and that a *fortiori* it is impossible to say that one would be better than the other.

What is striking when reading both Falk & Heckman (2009) and advocates of field experiments – such as Levitt & List (2009) – is that field studies and experiments are both very similar to theoretical models. They all share the same basic problem – they are built on rather artificial conditions and have difficulties with the trade-off between internal and external validity. The more artificial conditions, the more internal validity – but also less external validity. The more we rig experiments/field studies/models to avoid confounding factors, the less the conditions are reminiscent of the real target system. To that extent, Falk & Heckman are probably right in their comments on the discussion of the field vs. experiments in terms of realism – the nodal issue is not about that, but basically about how economists using different isolation strategies in different "nomological machines" attempt to learn about causal relationships. By contrast with Falk and Heckman and advocates of field experiments, as Steven Levitt and John List, I doubt the generalizability of *both* research strategies, because the probability is high that causal mechanisms are different in different contexts, and that lack of homogeneity/ stability/invariance does not give us warranted export licenses to the "real" societies or economies.

Experiments, field studies and the quest for external validity

If you mainly conceive of experiments or field studies as heuristic tools, the dividing line between, say, Falk & Heckman and Levitt & List, is probably difficult to perceive. But if we see experiments or field studies as theory tests or models that ultimately aspire to say something about the real target system, then the problem of external validity is central (and was for a long time also a key reason why behavioural economists had trouble getting their research results published).

Assume that you have examined how the work performance of Chinese workers, A, is affected by B ("treatment"). How can we extrapolate/ generalize to new samples outside the original population (e.g. to the US)? How do we know that any replication attempt "succeeds"? How do we know when these replicated experimental results can be said to justify inferences made in samples from the original population? If, for example, P(A|B) is the conditional density function for the original sample, and we are interested in doing an extrapolative prediction of E [P(A|B)], how can we know that the new sample's density function is identical with the original? Unless we can give some really good argument for this being the case, inferences built on P(A|B) is not really saying anything on that of the target system's P'(A|B).

This is the heart of the matter. External validity/extrapolation/generalization is founded on the assumption that we can make inferences based on P(A|B) that is exportable to other populations for which P'(A|B) applies. Sure, if one can convincingly show that P and P' are similar enough, the problems are perhaps surmountable. But arbitrarily just introducing functional specification restrictions of the type invariance/stability/homogeneity, is, at least for an epistemological realist far from satisfactory. And often it is – unfortunately – exactly this that I see when I take part of neoclassical economists' models/experiments/field studies.

By this I do not mean to say that empirical methods *per se* are so problematic that they can never be used. On the contrary, I am basically – though not without reservations – in favour of the increased use of experiments and field studies within economics. Not least as an alternative to completely barren bridge-less axiomatic-deductive theory models. My criticism is more about aspiration levels and what we believe we can achieve with our mediational epistemological tools and methods in the social sciences.

Many experimentalists claim that it is easy to replicate experiments under different conditions and therefore a *fortiori* easy to test the robustness of experimental results. But is it really that easy? If in the example given above, we run a test and find that our predictions were not correct – what can we conclude? That B "works" in China but not in the US? Or that B "works" in a backward agrarian society, but not in a post-modern service society? That B "worked" in the field study conducted in year 2008, but not in year 2015? Population selection is almost never simple. Had the problem of external validity only been about inference from sample to population, this would be no critical problem. But the really interesting inferences are those we try to make from specific labs/experiments/fields to specific real world situations/institutions/structures that we are interested in understanding or explaining. And then the population problem is more difficult to tackle.

Randomization – in search of a gold standard for evidence-based theories

Evidence-based theories and policies are highly valued nowadays. Randomization is supposed to best control for bias from unknown confounders. The received opinion is that evidence based on randomized experiments therefore is the best. More and more economists have also lately come to advocate randomization as the principal method for ensuring being able to make valid causal inferences.

Renowned econometrician Ed Leamer (2010) has responded to these allegations, maintaining that randomization is not sufficient, and that the hopes of a better empirical and quantitative macroeconomics are to a large extent illusory. Randomization promises more than it can deliver, basically because it requires assumptions that in practice are not possible to maintain:

> We economists trudge relentlessly toward Asymptopia, where data are unlimited and estimates are consistent, where the laws of large numbers apply perfectly and where the full intricacies of the economy are completely revealed. But it's a frustrating journey, since, no matter how far we travel, Asymptopia remains infinitely far away. Worst of all, when we feel pumped up with our progress, a tectonic shift

can occur, like the Panic of 2008, making it seem as though our long journey has left us disappointingly close to the State of Complete Ignorance whence we began.

The pointlessness of much of our daily activity makes us receptive when the Priests of our tribe ring the bells and announce a shortened path to Asymptopia ... We may listen, but we don't hear, when the Priests warn that the new direction is only for those with Faith, those with complete belief in the Assumptions of the Path. It often takes years down the Path, but sooner or later, someone articulates the concerns that gnaw away in each of us and asks if the Assumptions are valid ... Small seeds of doubt in each of us inevitably turn to despair and we abandon that direction and seek another ...

Ignorance is a formidable foe, and to have hope of even modest victories, we economists need to use every resource and every weapon we can muster, including thought experiments (theory), and the analysis of data from nonexperiments, accidental experiments, and designed experiments. We should be celebrating the small genuine victories of the economists who use their tools most effectively, and we should dial back our adoration of those who can carry the biggest and brightest and least-understood weapons. We would benefit from some serious humility, and from burning our "Mission Accomplished" banners. It's never gonna happen.

Part of the problem is that we data analysts want it all automated. We want an answer at the push of a button on a keyboard ... Faced with the choice between thinking long and hard versus pushing the button, the single button is winning by a very large margin.

> Let's not add a "randomization" button to our intellectual keyboards, to be pushed without hard reflection and thought.

Especially when it comes to questions of causality, randomization is nowadays considered some kind of "gold standard". But just as econometrics, randomization is basically a deductive method. Given the assumptions (such as manipulability, transitivity, Reichenbach probability principles, separability, additivity, linearity, etc.) these methods deliver deductive inferences. The problem, of course, is that we will never completely know when the assumptions are right. As Nancy Cartwright (2007) formulates it:

> We experiment on a population of individuals each of whom we take to be described (or 'governed') by the same *fixed causal structure* (albeit unknown) and *fixed probability measure* (albeit unknown). Our deductive conclusions depend on that very causal structure and probability. How do we know what individuals beyond those in our experiment this applies to? ... The [randomized experiment], with its vaunted rigor, takes us only a very small part of the way we need to go for practical knowledge. This is what disposes me to warn about the vanity of rigor in [randomized experiments].

Although randomization may contribute to controlling for confounding, it does not guarantee it, since genuine randomness presupposes infinite experimentation and we know all real experimentation is finite. And even if randomization may help to establish average causal effects, it says nothing of individual effects unless homogeneity is added to the list of assumptions.

Real target systems are seldom epistemically isomorphic to our axiomatic-deductive models/systems, and even if they were, we still have to argue for the external validity of the conclusions reached from within these epistemically convenient models/systems. Causal evidence generated by randomization procedures may be valid in "closed" models, but what we usually are interested in is causal evidence in the real target system we happen to live in.

So, when does a conclusion established in population X hold for target population Y? Usually only under very restrictive conditions! As Nancy Cartwright (2011) – succinctly summarizing the value of randomization – writes:

> But recall the logic of randomized control trials ... They are ideal for supporting 'it-works-somewhere' claims. But they are in no way ideal for other purposes; in particular they provide no better bases for extrapolating or generalising than knowledge that the treatment caused the outcome in any other individuals in any other circumstances ... And where no capacity claims obtain, there is seldom warrant for assuming that a treatment that works somewhere will work anywhere else. (The exception is where there is warrant to believe that the study population is a representative sample of the target population – and cases like this are hard to come by.)

Ideally controlled experiments (the benchmark even for natural and quasi experiments) tell us with certainty what causes what effects – but only given the right closures. Making appropriate extrapolations from (ideal, accidental, natural or quasi) experiments to different settings, populations or target systems, is not easy. "It works there" is no evidence for "it will work here." Causes deduced in an experimental setting still have to show that they come with an export-warrant to the target population/system. The causal background assumptions made have to be justified, and without licenses to export, the value of "rigorous" and "precise" methods is despairingly small.

Here I think Leamer's button metaphor is appropriate. Many advocates of randomization want to have deductively automated answers to fundamental causal questions. But to apply "thin" methods we have to have "thick" background knowledge of what's going on in the real world, and not in (ideally controlled) experiments. Conclusions can only be as certain as their premises – and that also goes for methods based on randomized experiments.

An interesting example that illustrates some of the problems with randomization – spillovers and the bridging of the micro-macro gap – was recently presented in an article by Pieter Gautier *et al.* (2012):

> In new research, we study a Danish job search assistance programme which, according to a randomised experiment, leads to large positive effects on exit rates to work ... We show, however, that because of spillover effects, a large-scale implementation will only marginally reduce unemployment without increasing welfare ...

> The empirical results suggest that considering both negative and positive spillover effects is important when evaluating the job search assistance programme. The Danish programme essentially increases the job search effort of participants by requiring them to make more job applications. The effect on vacancy supply is modest, so when participants send out more applications, this reduces the probability that a specific job application gets selected.

> It is often argued that randomised experiments are the golden standard for such evaluations. However, it is well know that a randomised experiment only provides a policy-relevant treatment effect when there are no spillovers between individuals. In the study discussed above, we have shown that spillovers can be substantial. Despite the success of a small-scale implementation of the programme at the micro level, we find it to be ineffective at the macro level. The results of our study are no exception.

So this example does pretty well explain one reason for randomized controlled trials not at all being the "gold standard" that it has lately often been portrayed as. Randomized controlled trials usually do not provide evidence that their results are exportable to other target systems. The almost religious belief with which its propagators portray it, cannot hide the fact that randomized controlled trials cannot be taken for granted to give *generalizable* results. That something works somewhere is no warranty for it to work for us or even that it works *generally*.

Econometrics and the difficult art of making it count

In an article that attracted much attention, renowned econometrician and Nobel laureate James Heckman (2005) writes (emphasis added):

> A model is a set of possible counterfactual worlds constructed under some rules. The rules may be laws of physics, the consequences of utility maximization, or the rules governing social interactions ... *A model is in the mind. As a consequence, causality is in the mind.*

Even though this is a standard view among econometricians, it is – at least from a realist point of view – rather untenable. The reason we as scientists are interested in causality is that it is a part of the way the world works. We *represent* the workings of causality in the real world by means of models, but that doesn't mean that causality is not a fact pertaining to relations and structures that exist in the real world. If it was only "in the mind," most of us couldn't care less.

The reason behind Heckman's and most other econometricians' nominalist-positivist view of science and models, is the belief that science can only deal with observable regularity patterns of a more or less lawlike kind. Only data matters, and trying to (ontologically) go beyond observed data in search of the underlying real factors and relations that generate the data is not admissible. All has to take place in the econometric mind's model since the real factors and relations according to the econometric methodology are beyond reach since they allegedly are both unobservable and immeasurable. This also means that instead of treating the model-based findings as interesting *clues* for digging deeper into real structures and mechanisms, they are treated as the *end points* of the investigation. Or as Asad Zaman (2012) puts it:

> Instead of taking it as a first step, as a clue to explore, conventional econometric methodology terminates at the discovery of a good fit ... Conventional econometric methodology is a failure because it is merely an attempt to find patterns in the data, without any tools to assess whether or not the given pattern reflects some real forces which shape the data.

David Freedman (2010) raises a similar critique:

> In my view, regression models are not a particularly good way of doing empirical work in the social sciences today, because the technique depends on knowledge that we do not have. Investigators who use the technique are not paying adequate attention to the connection – if any – between the models and the phenomena they are studying. Their conclusions may be valid for the computer code they have created, but the claims are hard to transfer from that microcosm to the larger world.

> Given the limits to present knowledge, I doubt that models can be rescued by technical fixes. Arguments about the theoretical merit of regression or the asymptotic behavior of specification tests for picking one version of a model over another seem like the arguments about how to build desalination plants with cold fusion and the energy source. The concept may be admirable, the technical details may be fascinating, but thirsty people should look elsewhere.

Most advocates of econometrics and regression analysis want to have deductively automated answers to fundamental causal questions. Econometricians think – as David Hendry expressed it in *Econometrics – alchemy or science?* (1993) – they "have found their Philosophers' Stone; it is called regression analysis and is used for transforming data into 'significant' results!" But as David Freedman (2010) poignantly notes – "Taking assumptions for granted is what makes statistical techniques into philosophers' stones." To apply "thin" methods we have to have "thick" background knowledge of what is going on in the real world, and not in idealized models. Conclusions can only be as certain as their premises – and that also applies to the quest for causality in econometrics and regression analysis.

Without requirements of depth, explanations most often do not have practical significance. Only if we search for and find fundamental structural causes, can we hopefully also take effective measures to remedy problems like e.g. mass unemployment, poverty, discrimination and underdevelopment. A social science must try to establish what relations exist between different phenomena and the systematic forces that operate within the different realms of reality. If econometrics is to progress, it has to abandon its outdated nominalist-positivist view of science and the belief that science can only deal with observable regularity patterns of a more or less law-like kind. Scientific theories ought to do more than just describe event-regularities and patterns – they also have to analyze and describe the mechanisms, structures, and processes that give birth to these patterns and eventual regularities.

Modern econometrics is fundamentally based on assuming – usually without any explicit justification – that we can gain causal knowledge by considering independent variables that may have an impact on the *variation* of a dependent variable. This is however, far from self-evident. Often the *fundamental* causes are *constant* forces that are not amenable to the kind of analysis econometrics supplies us with. Or as Stanley Lieberson (1985) has it:

> One can always say whether, in a given empirical context, a given variable or theory accounts for more variation than another. But it is almost certain that the variation observed is not universal over time and place. Hence the use of such a criterion first requires a conclusion about the variation over time and place in the dependent variable. If such an analysis is not forthcoming, the theoretical conclusion is undermined by the absence of information ...

Moreover, it is questionable whether one can draw much of a conclusion about causal forces from simple analysis of the observed variation ... To wit, it is vital that one have an understanding, or at least a working hypothesis, about what is causing the event per se; variation in the magnitude of the event will not provide the answer to that question.

Conclusion

Statistics and econometrics should not – as already Keynes (1973(1921)) argued – primarily be seen as means of inferring causality from observational data, but rather as descriptions of patterns of associations and correlations that we may use as *suggestions* of possible causal relations.

Causality in social sciences – and economics – can never solely be a question of statistical inference. Causality entails more than predictability, and to really in depth explain social phenomena require theory. Analysis of variation – the foundation of all econometrics – can never in itself reveal *how* these variations are brought about. First when we are able to tie actions, processes or structures to the statistical relations detected, can we say that we are getting at relevant explanations of causation. Too much in love with axiomatic-deductive modeling, neoclassical economists especially tend to forget that accounting for causation – *how* causes bring about their effects – demands deep subject-matter knowledge and acquaintance with the intricate fabrics and contexts.

.

On the use and misuse of theories and models in economics

Microfoundations – spectacularly useless and positively harmful

Most New Classical and "New Keynesian" macroeconomists today seem to subscribe to a methodological individualist view, according to which the only "rigorous," "acceptable," "well-grounded" or "secure" way to do macroeconomics, is to somehow reduce it to microeconomic analysis. Implementing a microfoundationalist programme, these economists believe that macroeconomics is both dispensable and/or basically reducible to microeconomics. Adhering – consciously or not – to a methodological individualist stance, macroeconomic facts are to be explained only in terms of facts about individual agents. Only when we have arrived at explaining macroeconomic phenomena by deriving them from explanatory primary microeconomic "deep parameters" like preferences, tastes, aspirations and beliefs of individuals, have we got adequate explanations.

But as economists, philosophers, historians and methodologists – such as e. g. John King (2012), Alan Nelson (1984), Roy Bhaskar (1989), John Searle (1996), Tony Lawson (1997), Wim Meeusen (2011), James Hartley (1997) and Kevin Hoover (2001, 2009, 2010a, 2010b) – have forcefully argued, there exist overwhelmingly strong reasons for being critical and doubtful *re* methodological individualism and reductionism and the urge for microfoundations of macroeconomics. In this chapter I want to elaborate on a couple of them.

Microfoundations today – on the history, significance and interpretation of earlier microfoundationalist programmes, cf. Weintraub (1979), Janssen (2006), Syll (2011), King (2012) and Hoover (2010b, 2013) – means more than anything else trying to *reduce* macroeconomics to microeconomics by building macroeconomic models assuming "rational expectations" and hyper-rational "representative agents" optimizing over time. Both are highly questionable assumptions. That a specific theory/method/approach has been established as *the* way of performing economic analysis in the economics community, is not a proof of its validity, as we will see.

The concept of rational expectations was first developed by John Muth (1961) and later applied to macroeconomics by Robert Lucas (1972). Those macroeconomic models building on rational expectations microfoundations that are used today among both New Classical and "New Keynesian" macroconomists, basically assume that people on average hold expectations that will be fulfilled. This makes the economist's analysis enormously simplistic, since it means that the model used by the economist is the same as the one people use to make decisions and forecasts of the future.

Rather than assuming that people on average have the same expectations, someone like Keynes for example, would argue that people often have different expectations and information, and that this constitutes the basic rational behind macroeconomic needs of coordination – something that is rather swept under the rug by the extremely simple-mindedness of assuming rational expectations in representative agents models. But if all actors are alike, why do they transact? Who do they transact with? The very reason for markets and exchange seems to slip away with the sister assumptions of representative agents and rational expectations.

Microfoundations – when microeconomic modeling becomes the message

Macroeconomic models building on rational expectations microfoundations impute beliefs to the agents that is not based on any real informational considerations, but simply stipulated to make the models mathematically-statistically tractable. Of course you can make assumptions based on tractability, but then you do also have to take into account the necessary trade-off in terms of the ability to make relevant and valid statements on the intended target system. Mathematical tractability cannot be the ultimate arbiter in science when it comes to modeling real world target systems. One could perhaps accept macroeconomic models building on rational expectations microfoundations if they had produced lots of verified predictions and good explanations. But they have done nothing of the kind. Therefore the burden of proof is on those macroeconomists who still want to use models built on these particular unreal assumptions.

Using models in science usually implies that simplifications have to be made. But it comes at a price. There is almost always a trade-off between rigour and analytical tractability on the one hand, and relevance and realism on the other. Modern Walrasian macroeconomic models err on the side of rigour and analytical tractability. They fail to meet Einstein's 'Not More So' criterion – thereby making macroeconomics less useful and more simplistic than necessary. Models should be as simple as possible – but 'Not More So.'

If you want the model to fit reality this ought to be rather self-evident. However, when confronting modern Walrasian macroeconomic model builders with this kind of critique, a common strategy used is to actually deny that there ever was any intention of being realistic – the sole purpose of the models are said to function as *bench-marks* against which to judge the real world we happen to live in. For someone devoted to the study of economic methodology it is difficult not to express surprise at this unargued and nonsensical view. This is nothing but a new kind of *Nirvana fallacy* – and why on earth should we consider it worthwhile and interesting to make evaluations of real economies based on abstract, imaginary, fantasy worlds? It's absolutely unwarranted from a scientific point of view. It's like telling physiologists to evaluate the human body from the perspective of unicorns – they would not take you seriously. And it is difficult from a critical realist point of view to come up with any reason whatsoever why we should judge these macroeconomic model builders differently.

In macroeconomic models building on rational expectations microfoundations – where agents are assumed to have complete knowledge of all of the relevant probability distribution functions – nothing really new happens, since they take for granted that people's decisions can be portrayed as being based on an existing probability distribution, which by definition implies the knowledge of every possible event (otherwise it is in a strict mathematical-statistically sense not really a probability distribution at all) that can be thought of taking place.

But in the real world, it is not possible to just assume that probability distributions are the right way to characterize, understand or explain acts and decisions made under uncertainty. When we simply do not know, when we have not got a clue, when genuine uncertainty prevails, macroeconomic models building on rational expectations microfoundations simply will not do. In those circumstances it is not a useful assumption. The main reason being that under those circumstances the future is not like the past, and henceforth, we cannot use the same probability distribution – if it at all exists – to describe both the past and future.

The future is not reducible to a known set of prospects. It is not like sitting at the roulette table and calculating what the future outcomes of spinning the wheel will be. We have to surpass macroeconomic models building on rational expectations microfoundations and instead try to build economics on a more realistic foundation – a foundation that encompasses both risk and genuine uncertainty.

Macroeconomic models building on rational expectations microfoundations emanates from the belief that to be scientific, economics has to be able to model individuals and markets in a stochastic-deterministic way. It's like treating individuals and markets as the celestial bodies studied by astronomers with the help of gravitational laws. Unfortunately, individuals, markets and entire economies are not planets moving in predetermined orbits in the sky.

To deliver macroeconomic models building on rational expectations microfoundations the economists have to constrain expectations on the individual and the aggregate level to be the same. If revisions of expectations take place, they typically have to take place in a known and pre-specified precise way. This squares badly with what we know to be true in real world, where fully specified trajectories of future expectations revisions are non-existent.

Further, most macroeconomic models building on rational expectations microfoundations are time-invariant and *a fortiori* give no room for any changes in expectations and their revisions. The only imperfection of knowledge they admit of is included in the error terms, error terms that are standardly assumed to be linearly additive and to have a given and known frequency distribution, so that the models can still fully pre-specify the future even when incorporating stochastic variables into the models.

In the real world there are many different expectations and these cannot be aggregated in macroeconomic models building on rational expectations microfoundations without giving rise to inconsistency. This is one of the main reasons for these models being modeled as representative agents models. But this is far from being a harmless approximation to reality. Even the smallest differences of expectations between agents would make these models inconsistent, so when they still show up they have to be considered "irrational".

It is not possible to adequately represent individuals and markets as having one single overarching probability distribution. Accepting that, does not imply that we have to end all theoretical endeavours and assume that all agents always act totally irrationally and only are analyzable within behavioural economics. Far from it. It means we acknowledge diversity and imperfection, and that macroeconomics has to be able to incorporate these empirical facts in its models.

Purpose-built assumptions made solely to secure a way of reaching deductively validated results in mathematical models, are of little value if they cannot be validated outside of the model. Assuming away problems – rather than solving them – is not a scientific approach. As Kevin Hoover (2010a:346) writes:

> The idea that macroeconomics not only needs microfoundations, but that microeconomics can replace macroeconomics completely is the dominant position in modern economics. No one, however, knows how to derive empirically relevant explanations of observable aggregate relations from the precise individual behaviors that generate them. Instead, the claims to have produced microfoundations are typically fleshed out with representative agent models in which a single agent treats the aggregates as objects of direct choice, playing by rules

that appear to follow the logic and mathematics of microeconomics ...

I accept idealization as a strategy of model building. But legitimate idealization requires that the idealized model capture the essence of the causal structure or underlying mechanisms at work. It is only on that basis that we can trust the model to analyze situations other than the data to hand ... Yet, the trick of using models appropriately is that we should either be able to set aside these particularities in reasoning or show that the results of interest are robust to the range of particular forms that we might reasonably assume ...

The essence of the criticism of the common strategies of reducing microeconomics to macroeconomics is that it is based in model building that mixes legitimate idealizations with non-ideal, particular modeling assumptions and then relies on those assumptions at critical junctures in providing the derivation of the macroeconomic relationships from microeconomic behaviors.

Microfounded macromodels should enable us to posit counterfactual questions about what would happen if some variable was to change in a specific way (hence the assumption of structural invariance, that purportedly enables the theoretical economist to do just that). But do they? Applying a "Lucas critique" on most microfounded macromodels, it is obvious that they fail. Changing "policy rules" cannot just be presumed not to influence investment and consumption behaviour and a *fortiori* technology, thereby contradicting the invariance assumption. Technology and tastes cannot live up to the status of an economy's deep and structurally stable Holy Grail. They too are part and parcel of an ever-changing and open economy.

Without export certificates, models and theories should be considered unsold. Unfortunately this understanding has not informed modern neoclassical economics, as can be seen by the profuse use of representative agent models. For quite some time now, it has been a

Microfoundations – spectacularly useless and positively harmful

common feature of modern neoclassical macroeconomics to use simple dynamic stochastic general equilibrium – DSGE – models where representative agents are supposed to act in a world characterized by complete knowledge, zero transaction costs and complete markets.

In these models, the actors are all identical. This has, of course, far-reaching analytical implications. Situations characterized by asymmetrical information – situations most of us consider to be innumerable – cannot arise in such models. If the aim is to build a macro-analysis from micro-foundations in this manner, the relevance of the procedure is highly questionable – Robert Solow (2010) even considered the claims made by protagonists of representative agent models "generally phony."

One obvious critique – cf. Syll (2001) – is that representative agent models do not incorporate distributional effects – effects that often play a decisive role in macroeconomic contexts. Investigations into the operations of markets and institutions usually find that there are overwhelming problems of coordination. These are difficult, not to say impossible, to analyze with the kind of Robinson Crusoe models that, e. g., real business cycle theorists employ and which exclude precisely those differences between groups of actors that are the driving force in many non-neoclassical analyses.

The choices of different individuals have to be shown to be coordinated and consistent. This is obviously difficult if the macroeconomic models do not give room for heterogeneous individuals (this lack of understanding the importance of heterogeneity is perhaps especially problematic for the modeling of real business cycles in dynamic stochastic general equilibrium models). Assuming away the heterogeneity that exists at an individual level by using representative agent models, are certainly more manageable, however, from a realist point of view, these models are also less relevant and have a lower explanatory potential. As Kevin Hoover (2009:405) writes:

> The irony of the program of microfoundations is that, in the name of preserving the importance of individual intentional states and preserving the individual economic agent as the foundation of economics, it fails to provide any intelligible connection between the individual and the aggregate.

On the use and misuse of theories and models in economics

Instead, it embraces the representative agent, which is as close to an untethered Hegelian World (or Macroeconomic) Spirit as one might fear in the microfoundationist's worst nightmare.

Or as Robert Gordon (2009:25-26) has it:

In the end, the problem with modern macro is that it contains too much micro and not enough macro. Individual representative agents assume complete and efficient markets and market clearing, while the models ignore the basic macro interactions implied by price stickiness, including macro externalities and coordination failures. In an economy-wide recession, most agents are not maximizing unconditional utility functions as in DSGE models but are maximizing, i.e., trying to make the best out of a bad situation, under biting income and liquidity constraints. Perceptive comments by others as cited above reject the relevance of modern macro to the current cycle of excess leveraging and subsequent deleveraging, because complete and efficient markets are assumed, and there is no room for default, bankruptcy, insolvency, and illiquidity.

Both the "Lucas critique" and Keynes' critique of econometrics argued that it was inadmissible to project history on the future. Consequently an economic policy cannot presuppose that what has worked before, will continue to do so in the future. That macroeconomic models could get hold of correlations between different "variables" was not enough. If they could not get at the causal structure that generated the data, they were not really "identified". Lucas himself drew the conclusion that the problem with unstable relations was to construct models with clear microfoundations, where forward-looking optimizing individuals and robust, deep, behavioural parameters are seen to be stable even to changes in economic policies.

The purported strength of New Classical and "New Keynesian" macroeconomics is that they have firm anchorage in preference based microeconomics, and especially the decisions taken by intertemporal utility maximizing "forward looking" individuals. To some of us, however, this has come at too high a price. The almost quasi-religious insistence that macroeconomics has to have microfoundations – without ever presenting neither ontological nor epistemological justifications for this claim – has put a blind eye to the weakness of the whole enterprise of trying to depict a complex economy based on an all-embracing representative agent equipped with superhuman knowledge, forecasting abilities and forward-looking rational expectations. It is as if – after having swallowed the sour grapes of the Sonnenschein-Mantel-Debreu-theorem – these economists want to resurrect the omniscient Walrasian auctioneer in the form of all-knowing representative agents equipped with rational expectations and assumed to somehow know the true structure of our model of the world. How that could even be conceivable is beyond imagination, given that the ongoing debate on microfoundations, if anything, shows that not even we, the economists, can come to agreement on a common model.

Microfoundations – Walrasian "Santa Claus" economics trying to get around Sonnenschein-Mantel-Debreu

Almost a century and a half after Léon Walras founded neoclassical general equilibrium theory, economists still have not been able to show that markets *move* economies *to* equilibria. What we do know is that unique Pareto-efficient equilibria do *exist*.

But what good does that do? As long as we cannot show, except under exceedingly unrealistic assumptions, that there are convincing reasons to suppose there are forces which lead economies to equilibria – the value of general equilibrium theory is next to nil. As long as we cannot really demonstrate that there are forces operating – under reasonable, relevant and at least mildly realistic conditions – at moving markets to equilibria, there cannot really be any sustainable reason for anyone to pay any interest or attention to this theory. A stability that can only be proved by assuming "Santa Claus" conditions is of no avail. Most people do not believe in Santa Claus. It is for kids. And for good reasons.

On the use and misuse of theories and models in economics

Simply assuming the problem away or continuing to model a world full of agents behaving as economists – "often wrong, but never uncertain" – and still not being able to show that the system under reasonable assumptions converges to equilibrium, is a gross misallocation of intellectual resources and time.

Here's what a leading microeconomist – Alan Kirman (1989:129) – writes on the issue:

> Starting from 'badly behaved' individuals, we arrive at a situation in which not only is aggregate demand a nice function but, by a result of Debreu, equilibrium will be 'locally unique'. Whilst this means that at least there is some hope for local stability, the real question is, can we hope to proceed and obtain global uniqueness and stability?

> The unfortunate answer is a categorical no! [The results of Sonnenchein (1972), Debreu (1974), Mantel (1976) and Mas Collel (1985)] shows clearly why any hope for uniqueness or stability must be unfounded ... There is no hope that making the distribution of preferences or income 'not to dispersed' or 'single peaked' will help us to avoid the fundamental problem.

> The idea that we should start at the level of the isolated individual is one which we may well have to abandon ... we should be honest from the outset and assert simply that *by assumption* we postulate that each sector of the economy behaves as one individual and not claim any spurious microjustification ...

> Economists therefore should not continue to make strong assertions about this behaviour based on so-called general equilibrium models which are, in reality, no more than special examples with no basis in economic theory as it stands.

Microfoundations – spectacularly useless and positively harmful

Kenneth Arrow (1968) argues in a similar vein against the kind of reductionism implied in the microfoundationalist attempts at redirecting economics:

> The economy is irreducible ... in the sense that no matter how the households are divided into two groups, an increase in the initial assets held by the members of one group can be used to make feasible an allocation which will make no one worse off and at least one individual in the second group better off.

> It is perhaps interesting to observe that "atomistic" assumptions concerning individual households and firms are not sufficient to establish the existence of equilibrium; "global" assumptions ... are also needed (though they are surely unexceptionable). Thus, a limit is set to the tendency implicit in price theory, particularly in its mathematical versions, to deduce all properties of aggregate behavior from assumptions about individual economic agents.

Getting around Sonnenschein-Mantel-Debreu using representative agents may be – as noted by Meeusen (2011) – very expedient from a purely formalistic point of view. But from a scientific point of view it is hardly relevant or realistic. As Rizvi (1994:363) maintains:

> The impact of SMD theory is quite general ... Its chief implication, in the authors view, is that the hypothesis of individual rationality, and the other assumptions made at the micro level, gives no guidance to an analysis of macro-level phenomena: the assumption of rationality or utility maximisation is not enough to talk about social regularities. This is a significant conclusion and brings the microfoundations project in GET [General Equilibrium Theory] to an end ... A theory based on micro principles or on appeals to them and which purports to analyse micro-level regularities *must* deal with aggregation; not doing so is not an option.

On the use and misuse of theories and models in economics

In microeconomics we know that (ideal) aggregation really presupposes homothetic an identical preferences, something that almost never exist in real economies – if they do, it means that you and multi-billionaire Richard Branson have the same preferences and that we after having had, e. g. a 99 % "haircut," still spend the same proportion of our incomes on, e. g. bread and butter, as before the massive income reduction.

To illustrate – following Nelson (1984) and Hoover (2001) – assume we have a very simple economy consisting of two consumers (i) trying to optimally choose consuming two commodities (c1 and c2) in two time periods by maximizing a logarithmic Cobb-Douglas utility function of the form $u^i = c^i1 + a^ic^i2$, given the (always satisfied) budget constraint $y = c^i1 + pc^i2$ (where y is income and p the price of commodity 2 in terms of the numéraire, commodity 1). Demand for commodity 1 is

(1) $c^i1 = y^i/(1 + a^i)$.

Aggregating (indicated by upper-case letters) the demand for commodity 1, we get

(2) $C1 = Y/(1 + a) = c^i1 + c^i2 = y^1/(1 + a^1) + y^2/(1 + a^2) = [y^1(1 + a^1) + y^2(1 + a^2)]/[(1 + a^1)(1 + a^2)] = [Y + a^1y^1 + a^2y^2]/[(1 + a^1)(1 + a^2)]$,

where the last equality follows from $Y = y^1 + y^2$. As can easily be seen, (1) and (2) are only of an identical form if all consumers have identical preferences – that is, $a^1 = a^2 = a$ – and homothetic utility functions yielding linear Engel curves, as e. g. the Cobb-Douglas utility function.

If these requirements are fulfilled, ideal aggregation from micro to macro can take place. Why? As Hoover (2001:79) puts it:

> In such circumstances, for a fixed aggregate income, redistributing that income among the individual consumers will not affect demands for individual goods and, therefore, will not affect relative prices ... and we can add up individual quantities to form economy-wide aggregates without loss of information.

However, if these patently unreal assumptions are *not* fulfilled, there is no guarantee of a straightforward and constant relation between individuals (micro) and aggregates (macro). The results given by these assumptions are *a fortiori* not robust and do not capture the underlying mechanisms at work in any real economy. And as if this impossibility of ideal aggregation was not enough, there are obvious problems also with the kind of microeconomic equilibrium that one tries to reduce macroeconomics to. Decisions of consumption and production are described as choices made by a single agent. But then, who sets the prices on the market? And how do we justify the assumption of universal consistency between the choices? Models that are critically based on particular and odd assumptions – and are neither robust nor congruent to real world economies – are of questionable value.

And is it really possible to describe and analyze all the deliberations and choices made by individuals in an economy? Does not the choice of an individual presuppose knowledge and expectations about choices of other individuals? It probably does, and this presumably helps to explain why representative agent models have become so popular in modern macroeconomic theory. They help to make the analysis more tractable.

One could justifiably argue that one might just as well accept that it is not possible to coherently reduce macro to micro, and accordingly that it is perhaps necessary to forswear microfoundations and the use of rational-agent models all together. Microeconomic reasoning has to build on macroeconomic presuppositions. Real individuals do not base their choices on operational general equilibrium models, but rather use simpler models. *If macroeconomics needs microfoundations it is equally necessary that microeconomics needs macrofoundations.*

On the impossibility of microfoundational reductionism

Alan Kirman (1992) maintains that the use of representative agent models is unwarranted and leads to conclusions that are usually both misleading and false. It is a fiction basically used by some macroeconomists to justify the use of equilibrium analysis and a kind of pseudo-microfoundations. Microeconomists are well aware that the conditions necessary to make aggregation to representative agents possible are not met in actual economies. As economic models become increasingly complex, their use also becomes less credible.

Already back in the 1930s, Keynes (1939) held a similar anti-reductionist view:

> I have called my theory a *general* theory. I mean by this that I am chiefly concerned with the behaviour of the economic system as a whole, – with aggregate incomes, aggregate profits, aggregate output, aggregate employment, aggregate investment, aggregate saving rather than with the incomes, profits, output, employment, investment and saving of particular industries, firms or individuals. And I argue that important mistakes have been made through extending to the system as a whole conclusions which have been correctly arrived at in respect of a part of it taken in isolation...

> Quite legitimately we regard an individual's income as independent of what he himself consumes and invests. But this, I have to point out, should not have led us to overlook the fact that the demand arising out of the consumption and investment of one individual is the source of the incomes of other individuals, so that incomes in general are not independent, quite the contrary, of the disposition of individuals to spend and invest; and since in turn the readiness of individuals to spend and invest depends on their incomes, a relationship is set up between aggregate savings and aggregate investment which can be very easily shown, beyond any possibility of reasonable dispute, to be one of exact and necessary equality. Rightly regarded this is a banale conclusion.

Microfoundations – spectacularly useless and positively harmful

Actually, Keynes way back in 1926 [Keynes 1933(1926)] more or less buried any ideas of microfoundations:

> The atomic hypothesis which has worked so splendidly in Physics breaks down in Psychics. We are faced at every turn with the problems of Organic Unity, of Discreteness, of Discontinuity – the whole is not equal to the sum of the parts, comparisons of quantity fails us, small changes produce large effects, the assumptions of a uniform and homogeneous continuum are not satisfied. Thus the results of Mathematical Psychics turn out to be derivative, not fundamental, indexes, not measurements, first approximations at the best; and fallible indexes, dubious approximations at that, with much doubt added as to what, if anything, they are indexes or approximations of.

Where "New Keynesian" and New Classical economists think they can rigorously deduce the aggregate effects of the acts and decisions of consumers and firms with their reductionist microfoundational methodology, they actually have to put a blind eye on the emergent properties that characterize all open social and economic systems. The interaction between animal spirits, trust, confidence, institutions etc., cannot be deduced or reduced to a question answerable on the individual level. Macroeconomic structures and phenomena have to be analyzed on their own terms.

Contrary to the microfoundational programme of Lucas *et consortes*, Keynes did not consider equilibrium as the self-evident axiomatic starting point for economic analysis. Actually it was the classical idea of equilibrium that had made economics blind to the obvious real fact that involuntary outcomes, such as unemployment, are a common feature of market economies – and Keynes wanted to develop a more realist alternative, breaking with the conception of economics as an equilibrium discipline.

Even if economies naturally presuppose individuals, it does not follow that we can infer or explain macroeconomic phenomena solely from knowledge of these individuals. Macroeconomics is to a large extent emergent and cannot be reduced to a simple summation of micro phenomena. Moreover, as we have already argued, even these microfoundations aren't immutable. Lucas and the new classical economists' deep parameters – "tastes" and "technology" – are not really the bedrock of constancy that they believe (pretend) them to be.

For Alfred Marshall economic theory was "an engine for the discovery of concrete truth". But where Marshall tried to describe the behaviour of a typical business with the concept "representative firm," his modern heirs do not at all try to describe how firms interplay with other firms in an economy. The economy is rather described "as if" consisting of one single giant firm/consumer/household – either by inflating the optimization problem of the individual to the scale of a whole economy, or by assuming that it's possible to aggregate different individuals' actions by a simple summation, since every type of actor is identical. But it would most probably be better if we just faced the fact that it is difficult to describe interaction and cooperation when there is essentially only one actor – instead of sweeping aggregation problems, fallacies of composition and emergence under the rag.

Those who want to build macroeconomics on microfoundations usually maintain that the only robust policies and institutions are those based on rational expectations and representative agents. But there is really no support for this conviction at all. On the contrary – if we want to have anything of interest to say on real economies, financial crisis and the decisions and choices real people make, it is high time to redirect macroeconomics away from constructing models building on representative agents and rational expectations-microfoundations. Since representative-agent-rational-expectations (RARE) microfounded macroeconomics has nothing to say about the real world and the economic problems out there, why should we care about it? The final court of appeal for macroeconomic models is the real world, and as long as no convincing justification is put forward for how the inferential bridging *de facto* is made, macroeconomic modelbuilding is little more than hand waving that give us rather little warrant for making inductive inferences from models to real world target systems. Even though equilibrium according to Lucas (Snowdon 1998:127) is considered "a property of the way we look at things, not a property of reality," this is hardly a tenable view. Analytical tractability should not be transformed into a methodological virtue. If substantive questions about the real world are being posed, it is the formalistic-mathematical representations utilized to analyze them that have to match reality, not the other way around.

Given that, I would say that macroeconomists – especially "Keynesian" ones – ought to be even *more* critical of the microfoundations dogma than they are. If macroeconomic models – no matter of what ilk – build on microfoundational *assumptions* of representative agents, rational expectations, market clearing and equilibrium, and we *know* that real people and markets cannot be expected to obey these assumptions, the warrants for supposing that conclusions or hypotheses of causally relevant mechanisms or regularities can be bridged, are obviously non-justifiable. Incompatibility between actual behaviour and the behaviour in macroeconomic models building on RARE microfoundations shows the futility of trying to represent real-world economies with models flagrantly at odds with reality.

In the conclusion to his book *Models of Business Cycles* Robert Lucas (1987:66-108) (in)famously wrote:

> It is remarkable and, I think, instructive fact that in nearly 50 years that Keynesian tradition has produced not one useful model of the individual unemployed worker, and no rationale for unemployment insurance beyond the observation that, in common with countercyclical cash grants to corporations or to anyone else, it has the effects of increasing the total volume of spending at the right times. By dogmatically insisting that unemployment be classed as 'involuntary' this tradition simply cut itself off from serious thinking about the actual options unemployed people are faced with, and hence from learning anything about how the alternative social arrangements might improve these options…

> If we are honest, we will have to face the fact that at any given time there will be phenomena that are well-understood from the point of view of the economic theory we have, and other phenomena that are not. We will be tempted, I am sure, to relieve the discomfort induced by discrepancies

between theory and facts by saying the ill-understood facts are the province of some other, different kind of economic theory. Keynesian 'macroeconomics' was, I think, a surrender (under great duress) to this temptation. It led to the abandonment, for a class of problems of great importance, of the use of the only 'engine for the discovery of truth' that we have in economics.

Thanks to latter-day Lucasian New-Classical-New-Keynesian-RARE-microfoundations-economists, we are supposed not to – as our "primitive" ancestors – use that archaic term 'macroeconomics' anymore (with the possible exception of warning future economists not to give in to "discomfort".) Being intellectually heavily indebted to the man who invented macroeconomics – Keynes – I firmly decline to concur.

Microfoundations – and *a fortiori* rational expectations and representative agents – serve a particular theoretical purpose. And as the history of macroeconomics during the last thirty years has shown, the Lucasian microfoundations programme for macroeconomics is only methodologically consistent within the framework of a (deterministic or stochastic) general equilibrium analysis. In no other context has it been considered *possible* to incorporate this kind of microfoundations – with its "forward-looking optimizing individuals" – into macroeconomic models.

This is of course not by accident. General equilibrium theory is basically nothing else than an endeavour to consistently generalize the microeconomics of individuals and firms on to the macroeconomic level of aggregates. *But it obviously does not work.* The analogy between microeconomic behaviour and macroeconomic behaviour is misplaced. Empirically, science-theoretically and methodologically, neoclassical microfoundations for macroeconomics are defective. Tenable foundations for macroeconomics really have to be sought for elsewhere.

Microfounded DSGE models – spectacularly useless and positively harmful

Economists working within the Post Keynesian tradition have always maintained that there is a strong risk that people may find themselves unemployed in a market economy. And, of course, unemployment is also something that can take place in microfounded DSGE models – but the mechanism in these models is of a fundamentally different kind.

In the basic DSGE models the labour market is always *cleared* – responding to a changing interest rate, expected life time incomes, or real wages, the representative agent maximizes the utility function by varying her labour supply, money holding and consumption over time. Most importantly – if the real wage somehow deviates from its "equilibrium value," the representative agent adjust her labour supply, so that when the real wage is higher than its "equilibrium value", labour supply is increased, and when the real wage is below its "equilibrium value", labour supply is decreased.

In this model world, unemployment is always an optimal choice to changes in the labour market conditions. Hence, unemployment is totally voluntary. To be unemployed is something one optimally chooses to be.

Although this picture of unemployment as a kind of self-chosen optimality, strikes most people as utterly ridiculous, there are also, unfortunately, a lot of neoclassical economists out there who still think that price and wage rigidities are the prime movers behind unemployment. What is even worse is that some of them even think that these rigidities are the reason John Maynard Keynes gave for the high unemployment of the Great Depression. This is of course pure nonsense. For although Keynes, in *General Theory,* devoted substantial attention to the subject of wage and price rigidities, he certainly *did not* hold this view. That's rather the view of microfounded DSGE modelers, explaining variations in employment (and *a fortiori* output) with assuming nominal wages being more flexible than prices – disregarding the lack of empirical evidence for this rather counterintuitive assumption.

People calling themselves "New Keynesians" ought to be rather embarrassed by the fact that the kind of microfounded DSGE models they use, cannot incorporate such a basic fact of reality as involuntary unemployment. Of course, working with representative agent models, this should come as no surprise. The kind of unemployment that occurs is voluntary, since it is only adjustments of the hours of work that these optimizing agents make to maximize their utility.

Kevin Hoover (2001:82-86) – who has been scrutinizing the microfoundations programme for now more than 25 years – writes:

> Given what we know about representative-agent models, there is not the slightest reason for us to think that the conditions under which they should work are fulfilled. The claim that representative-agent models provide microfundations succeeds only when we steadfastly avoid the fact that representative-agent models are just as aggregative as old-fashioned Keynesian macroeconometric models. They do not solve the problem of aggregation; rather they assume that it can be ignored. While they appear to use the mathematics of microeconomis, the subjects to which they apply that microeconomics are aggregates that do not belong to any agent. There is no agent who maximizes a utility function that represents the whole economy subject to a budget constraint that takes GDP as its limiting quantity. This is the simulacrum of microeconomics, not the genuine article...
>
> [W]e should conclude that what happens to the microeconomy is relevant to the macroeconomy but that macroeconomics has its own modes of analysis ... [I]t is almost certain that macroeconomics cannot be euthanized or eliminated. It shall remain necessary for the serious economist to switch back and forth between microeconomics and a relatively autonomous macroeconomics depending upon the problem in hand.

Alternatives to microfoundations

Defenders of microfoundations – and its concomitant rational expectations equipped representative agent's intertemporal optimization – often argue as if sticking with simple representative agent macroeconomic models doesn't impart a bias to the analysis. It's difficult not to reject such an unsubstantiated view.

Economists defending the microfoundationalist programme often also maintain that there are no methodologically coherent alternatives to microfoundations modeling – economic models based on the choices and acts of individuals is the only scientific game in town. That allegation is of course difficult to evaluate, but as argued in this book, the kind of miocrofoundationalist macroeconomics that New Classical economists and "New Keynesian" economists are pursuing, is certainly *not* methodologically coherent. And that ought to be rather embarrassing for those ilks of macroeconomists to whom axiomatics and deductivity is the hallmark of science *tout court*.

The fact that Lucas introduced rational expectations as a consistency axiom is not really an argument for why we should accept it as an acceptable assumption in a theory or model purporting to explain real macroeconomic processes. And although virtually any macroeconomic empirical claim is contestable, the same goes for microeconomics.

Of course there are alternatives to neoclassical general equilibrium microfoundations – behavioural economics and Frydman & Goldberg's (2007) "imperfect knowledge" economics being two noteworthy examples that easily come to mind. And for those who have not forgotten the history of our discipline – and who have not bought the sweet-water nursery tale of Lucas *et consortes* that Keynes was not "serious thinking" – it can easily be seen that there exists a macroeconomic tradition inspired by Keynes that has preciously little to do with any New Synthesis or "New Keynesianism".

Its ultimate building-block is the perception of genuine uncertainty and that people often "simply do not know". Real actors cannot know everything and their acts and decisions are not simply possible to sum or aggregate without the economist risking to succumb to the fallacy of composition. Instead of basing macroeconomics on unreal and unwarranted generalizations of microeconomic behaviour and relations, it is far better to accept the ontological fact that the future to a large extent is uncertain, and rather conduct macroeconomics on this fact of reality.

Conclusion

Assuming instant and unmodeled market clearing and/or approximating aggregate behaviour with unrealistically heroic assumptions of intertemporally optimizing rational-expectations-representative-agents, just will not do. The assumptions made, sur-reptitiously eliminate the very phenomena we want to study: uncertainty, disequilibrium, structural instability and problems of aggregation and coordination between different individuals and groups. Reducing macroeconomics to microeconomics, and microeconomics to refinements of hyper-rational Bayesian deductivist models, is not a viable way forward. It will only sentence to irrelevance the most interesting real world economic problems. Murder is probably the only way of reducing biology to chemistry – and disregarding Sonnenschein-Mantel-Debreu and trying to reduce macroeconomics to Walrasian general equilibrium microeconomics – basically means committing the same crime.

Commenting on the state of standard modern macroeconomics, Willem Buiter (2009) argues that neither New Classical nor "New Keynesian" microfounded DSGE macro models has helped us foresee, understand or craft solutions to the problems of today's economies:

> Most mainstream macroeconomic theoretical innovations since the 1970s... have turned out to be self-referential, inward-looking distractions at best. Research tended to be motivated by the internal logic, intellectual sunk capital and aesthetic puzzles of established research programmes rather than by a powerful desire to understand how the economy works...

Microfoundations – spectacularly useless and positively harmful

> Both the New Classical and New Keynesian complete markets macroeconomic theories not only did not allow questions about insolvency and illiquidity to be answered. They did not allow such questions to be asked...

> Charles Goodhart, who was fortunate enough not to encounter complete markets macroeconomics and monetary economics during his impressionable, formative years, but only after he had acquired some intellectual immunity, once said of the Dynamic Stochastic General Equilibrium approach which for a while was the staple of central banks' internal modelling: "It excludes everything I am interested in". He was right. It excludes everything relevant to the pursuit of financial stability.

Buiter's verdict is a worrying confirmation of neoclassical mainstream macroeconomics becoming more and more a "waste of time". Why do these economists waste their time and efforts on it? Besides aspirations of being published, Frank Hahn (2005) probably gave the truest answer, when interviewed on the occasion of his 80th birthday, he confessed that some economic assumptions didn't really say anything about "what happens in the world," but still had to be considered very good "because it allows us to get on this job".

The real macroeconomic challenge is to accept uncertainty and still try to explain why economic transactions take place – instead of simply conjuring the problem away by assuming uncertainty to be reducible to stochastic risk and disregarding the obvious ontological and methodological problems inherent in the individualist-reductionist microfoundations programme. That is scientific cheating. And it has been going on for too long now.

The Keynes-inspired building-blocks are there. But it is admittedly a long way to go before the whole construction is in place. But the sooner we are intellectually honest and ready to admit that modern neoclassical macroeconomics and its microfoundationalist programme has come to way's end – the sooner we can redirect our aspirations to more fruitful endeavours.

On the use and misuse of theories and models in economics

Economics textbooks – anomalies and transmogrification of truth

Theories are difficult to directly confront with reality. Economists therefore build models of their theories. Those models are representations that are directly examined and manipulated to indirectly say something about the target systems.

The obvious shortcoming of the basically epistemic – rather than ontological – neoclassical modeling approach is that similarity or resemblance *tout court* do not guarantee that the correspondence between model and target is interesting, relevant, revealing or somehow adequate in terms of mechanisms, causal powers, capacities or tendencies. No matter how many convoluted refinements of concepts made in the model, if the successive approximations do not result in models similar to reality in the appropriate respects – such as structure, isomorphism etc. – the surrogate system becomes a substitute system that does not bridge to the world but rather misses its target.

Many of the model assumptions made by neoclassical economics are *restrictive* rather than *harmless* and could *a fortiori* anyway not in any sensible meaning be considered approximations at all.

Below I will give four examples from neoclassical economics textbooks – on wage rigidities, the law of demand, revealed preferences, and expected utility – amply justifying this rather harsh judgment. In doing this, I also hope to contribute to the ongoing and necessary work on constructing a deprogramming manual for survivors of undergraduate courses in neoclassical economics.

On the use and misuse of theories and models in economics

On Keynes and wage rigidity

Among intermediate neoclassical macroeconomics textbooks, Charles Jones's textbook *Macroeconomics* (2nd ed, W W Norton, 2010) stands out as perhaps one of the better alternatives. Unfortunately it also contains some utter nonsense! In a chapter on "The Labor Market, Wages, and Unemployment" Jones writes:

> The point of this experiment is to show that *wage rigidities* can lead to large movements in employment. Indeed, they are the reason John Maynard Keynes gave, in *The General Theory of Employment, Interest, and Money* (1979 (1936)), for the high unemployment of the Great Depression.

This is of course pure nonsense. For although Keynes in *General Theory* devoted substantial attention to the subject of wage rigidities, he certainly *did not* hold the view that wage rigidities were "the reason ... for the high unemployment of the Great Depression."

Since unions/workers, contrary to classical assumptions, make wage-bargains in nominal terms, they will – according to Keynes – accept lower real wages caused by higher prices, but resist lower real wages caused by lower nominal wages. However, Keynes held it incorrect to attribute "cyclical" unemployment to this diversified agent behaviour. During the depression money wages fell significantly and – as Keynes noted – unemployment still grew. Thus, even when nominal wages are lowered, they do not generally lower unemployment.

In any specific labour market, lower wages could, of course, raise the demand for labour. But a general reduction in money wages would leave real wages more or less unchanged. The reasoning of the classical economists was, according to Keynes, a flagrant example of the "fallacy of composition." Assuming that since unions/workers in a specific labour market could negotiate real wage reductions via lowering nominal wages, unions/workers in general could do the same, the classics confused micro with macro.

Lowering nominal wages could not – according to Keynes – clear the labour market. Lowering wages – and possibly prices – could, perhaps, lower interest rates and increase investment. But to Keynes it would be much easier to achieve that effect by increasing the money supply. In any case, wage reductions was not seen by Keynes as a general substitute for an expansionary monetary or fiscal policy.

Even if potentially positive impacts of lowering wages exist, there are also more heavily weighing negative impacts – management-union relations deteriorating, expectations of on-going lowering of wages causing delay of investments, debt deflation, etc..

So, what Keynes actually did argue in *General Theory*, was that the classical proposition that lowering wages would lower unemployment and ultimately take economies out of depressions, was ill-founded and basically wrong.

To Keynes, flexible wages would only make things worse by leading to erratic price-fluctuations. The basic explanation for unemployment is insufficient aggregate demand, and that is mostly determined outside the labour market.

To mainstream neoclassical theory the kind of unemployment that occurs is voluntary, since it is only adjustments of the hours of work that these optimizing agents make to maximize their utility. Keynes on the other hand writes in *General Theory*:

> The classical school [maintains that] while the demand for labour at the existing money-wage may be satisfied before everyone willing to work at this wage is employed, this situation is due to an open or tacit agreement amongst workers not to work for less, and that if labour as a whole would agree to a reduction of money-wages more employment would be forthcoming. If this is the case, such unemployment, though apparently involuntary, is not strictly so, and ought to be included under the above category of 'voluntary' unemployment due to the effects of collective bargaining, etc....

On the use and misuse of theories and models in economics

The classical theory... is best regarded as a theory of distribution in conditions of full employment. So long as the classical postulates hold good, unemployment, which is in the above sense involuntary, cannot occur. Apparent unemployment must, therefore, be the result either of temporary loss of work of the 'between jobs' type or of intermittent demand for highly specialised resources or of the effect of a trade union 'closed shop' on the employment of free labour. Thus writers in the classical tradition, overlooking the special assumption underlying their theory, have been driven inevitably to the conclusion, perfectly logical on their assumption, that apparent unemployment (apart from the admitted exceptions) must be due at bottom to a refusal by the unemployed factors to accept a reward which corresponds to their marginal productivity...

Obviously, however, if the classical theory is only applicable to the case of full employment, it is fallacious to apply it to the problems of involuntary unemployment – if there be such a thing (and who will deny it?). The classical theorists resemble Euclidean geometers in a non-Euclidean world who, discovering that in experience straight lines apparently parallel often meet, rebuke the lines for not keeping straight – as the only remedy for the unfortunate collisions which are occurring. Yet, in truth, there is no remedy except to throw over the axiom of parallels and to work out a non-Euclidean geometry. Something similar is required to-day in economics. We need to throw over the second postulate of the classical doctrine and to work out the behaviour of a system in which involuntary unemployment in the strict sense is possible.

Unfortunately, Jones's macroeconomics textbook is not the only one containing this kind of utter nonsense on Keynes. Similar distortions of Keynes's views can be found in, e. g., the economics textbooks of the "New Keynesian" – a grotesque misnomer – Greg Mankiw. How is this possible? Probably because these economists have but a very superficial

98

acquaintance with Keynes's own works, and rather depend on second-hand sources like Hansen, Samuelson, Hicks and the likes. Fortunately there is a solution to the problem. Keynes's books are still in print. Read them!

The Law of Demand and the Sonnenschein-Mantel-Debreu theorem

As is well-known, Keynes used to criticize the more traditional economics for making the *fallacy of composition*, which basically consists of the false belief that the whole is nothing but the sum of its parts. Keynes argued that in the society and in the economy this was not the case, and that *a fortiori* an adequate analysis of society and economy couldn't proceed by just adding up the acts and decisions of individuals. The whole is more than a sum of parts.

This fact shows up already when orthodox – neoclassical – economics tries to argue for the existence of *The Law of Demand* – when the price of a commodity falls, the demand for it will increase – on the aggregate.

In one of the most used undergraduate textbook in economics used today, Greg Mankiw's and Mark Taylor's *Economics* (p. 70-71), we read:

> Because the quantity demanded falls as the price rises and rises as the price falls, we say that the quantity demanded is negatively related to the price. This relationship between price and quantity demanded is true for most goods in the economy and, in fact, is so pervasive that economists call it the law of demand: other things equal, when the price of a good rises, the quantity demanded of the good falls, and when the price falls, the quantity demanded rises. ...

> To analyse how markets work, we need to determine the market demand, which is the sum of all the individual demands for a particular good or service. ...

> The market demand curve shows how the total quantity demanded of a good varies as the price of the good varies,

while all the other factors that affect how much consumers want to buy, such as income and taste, amongst other things, are held constant.

But although it may be said that one succeeds in establishing The Law for single individuals, it is a well-established fact – firmly established already in 1976 in the *Sonnenschein-Mantel-Debreu theorem* – that it is not possible to extend The Law of Demand to apply on the market level, unless one makes ridiculously unrealistic assumptions such as individuals all having *homothetic preferences* – which actually implies that all individuals have *identical* preferences.

This can only be conceivable if there is in essence only one actor – the (in)famous *representative actor*. So, yes, it is possible to generalize The Law of Demand – as long as we assume that on the aggregate level there was only one commodity and one actor. What a generalization! Does this sound reasonable? Of course not. This is – again – pure nonsense!

How has neoclassical economics reacted to this devastating finding? Judging from how Mankiw, Taylor and hordes of other mainstream neoclassical economists handle it, basically by looking the other way, ignoring it and hoping that no one sees that the emperor is naked.

Having gone through a handful of the most frequently used textbooks of economics at the undergraduate level today, I can only conclude that the models that are presented in these modern neoclassical textbooks try to describe and analyze complex and heterogeneous real economies with a single rational-expectations-robot-imitation-representative-agent.

That is, with something that has absolutely nothing to do with reality. And – worse still – something that is not even amenable to the kind of general equilibrium analysis that they are thought to give a foundation for, since Hugo Sonnenschein (1972) , Rolf Mantel (1976) and Gérard Debreu (1974) *unequivocally* showed that there did not exist any condition by which assumptions on individuals would guarantee neither stability nor uniqueness of the equilibrium solution.

So what modern economics textbooks present to students are really models built on the assumption that an entire economy can be modeled as a representative actor and that this is a valid procedure. But it is not, as the Sonnenschein-Mantel-Debreu theorem irrevocably has shown.

Of course one could say that it is too difficult on undergraduate levels to show why the procedure is right and to defer it to master and doctoral courses. It could justifiably be reasoned that way – if what you teach your students is true, if The Law of Demand is generalizable to the market level and the representative actor is a valid modeling abstraction! But in this case it's demonstrably known to be false, and therefore this is nothing but a case of scandalous intellectual dishonesty. It's like telling your students that 2 + 2 = 5 and hope that they will never run into Peano's axioms of arithmetics.

For almost forty years neoclassical economics itself has lived with a theorem that shows the impossibility of extending the microanalysis of consumer behaviour to the macro level (unless making patently and admittedly insane assumptions). Still after all these years pretending in their textbooks that this theorem does not exist – none of the textbooks I investigated even mention the existence of the Sonnenschein-Mantel-Debreu theorem – is really outrageous.

Revealed preferences and the revolution that was called off

In 1938 Paul Samuelson offered a replacement for the then accepted theory of utility. The cardinal utility theory was discarded with the following words: "The discrediting of utility as a psychological concept robbed it of its possible virtue as an explanation of human behaviour in other than a circular sense, revealing its emptiness as even a construction" (1938, 61). According to Samuelson, the ordinalist revision of utility theory was, however, not drastic enough. The introduction of the concept of a marginal rate of substitution was considered "an artificial convention in the explanation of price behavior" (1938, 62). One ought to analyze the consumer's behaviour without having recourse to the concept of utility at all, since this did not correspond to directly observable phenomena. The old theory was criticized mainly from a methodological point of view, in that it used non-observable concepts and propositions.

The new theory should avoid this and thereby shed "the last vestiges of utility analysis" (1938, 62). Its main feature was a consistency postulate which said "if an individual selects batch one over batch two, he does not at the same time select two over one" (1938, 65). From this "perfectly clear" postulate and the assumptions of given demand functions and that all income is spent, Samuelson in (1938) and (1938a), could derive all the main results of ordinal utility theory (single-valuedness and homogeneity of degree zero of demand functions, and negative semi-definiteness of the substitution matrix).

In 1948 Samuelson no longer considered his "revealed preference" approach a new theory. It was then seen as a means of revealing consistent preferences and enhancing the acceptability of the ordinary ordinal utility theory by showing how one could construct an individual's indifference map by purely observing his market behaviour. Samuelson concluded his article by saying that "[t]he whole theory of consumer's behavior can thus be based upon operationally meaningful foundations in terms of revealed preference" (1948, 251). As has been shown lately, this is true only if we inter alia assume the consumer to be rational and to have unchanging preferences that are complete, asymmetrical, non-satiated, strictly convex, and transitive (or continuous). The theory, originally intended as a substitute for the utility theory, has, as Houthakker clearly notes, "tended to become complementary to the latter" (1950, 159).

Only a couple of years later, Samuelson held the view that he was in a position "to complete the programme begun a dozen years ago of arriving at the full empirical implications for demand behaviour of the most general ordinal utility analysis" (1950, 369). The introduction of Houthakker's amendment assured integrability, and by that the theory had according to Samuelson been "brought to a close" (1950, 355). Starting "from a few logical axioms of demand consistency ... [one] could derive the whole of the valid utility analysis as corollaries" (1950, 370). Since Samuelson had shown the "complete logical equivalence" of revealed preference theory with the regular "ordinal preference approach," it follows that "in principle there is nothing to choose between the formulations" (1953, 1). According to Houthakker (1961, 709), the aim of the revealed preference approach is "to formulate equivalent systems of axioms on preferences and on demand functions."

But if this is all, what has revealed preference theory then achieved? As it turns out, ordinal utility theory and revealed preference theory are – as Wong puts it – "not two different theories; at best, they are two different ways of expressing the same set of ideas" (2006, 118). And with regard to the theoretically solvable problem, we may still concur with Hicks that "there is in practice no direct test of the preference hypothesis" (1956, 58).

Sippel's experiments showed "a considerable number of violations of the revealed preference axioms" (1997, 1442) and that from a descriptive point of view – as a theory of consumer behaviour – the revealed preference theory was of a very limited value.

Today it seems as though the proponents of revealed preference theory have given up the original 1938-attempt at building a theory on nothing else but observable facts, and settled instead on the 1950-version of establishing "logical equivalences."

Mas-Collel et al. concludes their presentation of the theory by noting that "for the special case in which choice is defined for all subsets of X [the set of alternatives], a theory based on choice satisfying the weak axiom is completely equivalent to a theory of decision making based on rational preferences" (1995, 14).

Kreps holds a similar view, pointing to the fact that revealed preference theory is "consistent with the standard preference-based theory of consumer behavior" (1990, 30).

The theory of consumer behavior has been developed in great part as an attempt to justify the idea of a downward-sloping demand curve. What forerunners like e.g. Cournot (1838) and Cassel (1899) did was merely to *assert* this law of demand. The utility theorists tried to *deduce* it from axioms and postulates on individuals' economic behaviour. Revealed preference theory tried to build a new theory and to put it in operational terms, but ended up with just giving a theory logically equivalent to the old one. As such it also shares its shortcomings of being empirically nonfalsifiable and of being based on unrestricted universal statements.

As Kornai (1971, 133) remarked, "the theory is empty, tautological. The theory reduces to the statement that in period t the decision-maker chooses what he prefers ... The task is to explain *why* he chose precisely this alternative rather than another one." Further, pondering Amartya Sen's verdict of the revealed preference theory as essentially underestimating "the fact that man is a social animal and his choices are not rigidly bound to his own preferences only" (1982, 66) and Georgescu-Roegen's (1966, 192-3) apt description, a harsh assessment of what the theory accomplished should come as no surprise:

> Lack of precise definition should not... disturb us in moral sciences, but improper concepts constructed by attributing to man faculties which he actually does not possess, should. And utility is such an improper concept... [P]erhaps, because of this impasse... some economists consider the approach offered by the theory of choice as a great progress ... This is simply an illusion, because even though the postulates of the theory of choice do not use the terms 'utility' or 'satisfaction', their discussion and acceptance require that they should be translated into the other vocabulary... A good illustration of the above point is offered by the ingenious theory of the consumer constructed by Samuelson.

Nothing lost, nothing gained!

When talking of determining people's preferences through observation, Hal Varian in his intermediate microeconomics textbook, for example, has "to *assume* that the preferences will remain unchanged" and adopts "the convention that... the underlying preferences... are known to be strictly convex." He further *postulates* that the "consumer is an optimizing consumer." If we are "willing to add more *assumptions* about consumer preferences, we get more precise estimates about the shape of indifference curves" (2006, 119-123, author's italics). Given these assumptions, and that the observed choices satisfy the consistency postulate as amended by Houthakker, one can always construct preferences that "could have generated the observed choices." This does not, however, prove that the constructed preferences really generated the observed choices, "we can only show that observed behavior is not inconsistent with the statement. We can't prove that the economic model is correct."

Just as the Sonnenschein-Mantel-Debreu theorem, the case of revealed preference theory, turns out to be a splendid example of how unsuccessful have been the attempts of mainstream economics theory to deduce a law of demand from the neoclassical postulates of rational choice – and of the rather intellectually dishonest efforts at shoving foundational problems under the rug in mainstream economics textbooks.

Expected utility, non-ergodicity and the Kelly criterion

Although the expected utility theory is obviously both theoretically and descriptively inadequate, colleagues and microeconomics textbook writers all over the world gladly continue to use it, as though its deficiencies were unknown or unheard of.

Not even Robert Frank (2010:208) – in one of my favourite intermediate textbooks on microeconomics manages to get it quite right on this issue:

> As a general rule, human nature obviously prefers certainty to risk. At the same time, however, risk is an inescapable part of the environment. People naturally want the largest possible gain and the smallest possible risk, but most of the time we are forced to trade risk and gain off against one another. When choosing between two risky alternatives, we are forced to recognize this trade-off explicitly. In such cases, we cannot escape the cognitive effort required to reach a sensible decision. But when one of the alternatives is riskless, it is often easier simply to choose it and not

waste too much effort on the decision. What this pattern of behavior fails to recognize, however, is that choosing a sure win of $30 over an 80 percent chance to win $45 does precious little to reduce any of the uncertainty that really matters in life.

On the contrary, *when only small sums of money are at stake, a compelling case can be made that the only sensible strategy is to choose the alternative with the highest expected value.* The argument for this strategy ... rests on the law of large numbers. Here, the law tells us that if we take a large number of independent gambles and pool them, we can be very confident of getting almost exactly the sum of their expected values. As a decision maker, the trick is to remind yourself that each small risky choice is simply part of a much larger collection. After all, it takes the sting out of an occasional small loss to know that following any other strategy would have led to a virtually certain large loss.

To illustrate, consider again the choice between the sure gain of $30 and the 80 percent chance to win $45, and suppose you were confronted with the equivalent of one such choice each week. Recall that the gamble has an expected value of $36, $6 more than the sure thing. By always choosing the "risky" alternative, your expected gain -- over and beyond the gain from the sure alternative -- will be $312 each year. Students who have had an introductory course in probability can easily show that the probability you would have come out better by choosing the sure alternative in any year is less than 1 percent. *The long-run opportunity cost of following a risk-averse strategy for decisions involving small outcomes is an almost sure LOSS of considerable magnitude.* By thinking of your problem as that of choosing a policy for dealing with a large number of choices of the same type, a seemingly risky strategy is transformed into an obviously very safe one.

Economics textbooks – anomalies and transmogrification of truth

What Frank – and other mainstream textbook authors – tries to do in face of the obvious behavioural inadequacies of the expected utility theory, is to marginally mend it. But that cannot be the right attitude when facing scientific anomalies. When models are plainly wrong, you'd better replace them!

Daniel Kahneman [2011:113] writes – in *Thinking, Fast and Slow* – that expected utility theory is seriously flawed since it does not take into consideration the basic fact that people's choices are influenced by *changes* in their wealth. Where standard microeconomic theory assumes that preferences are stable over time, Kahneman and other behavioural economists have forcefully again and again shown that preferences aren't fixed, but vary with different reference points. How can a theory that doesn't allow for people having different reference points from which they consider their options have an almost axiomatic status within economic theory?

> The mystery is how a conception of the utility of outcomes that is vulnerable to such obvious counterexamples survived for so long. I can explain it only by a weakness of the scholarly mind... I call it theory-induced blindness: once you have accepted a theory and used it as a tool in your thinking it is extraordinarily difficult to notice its flaws... You give the theory the benefit of the doubt, trusting the community of experts who have accepted it... But they did not pursue the idea to the point of saying, "This theory is seriously wrong because it ignores the fact that utility depends on the history of one's wealth, not only present wealth."

On a more economic-theoretical level, information theory – and especially the so called the Kelly criterion– also highlights the problems concerning the neoclassical theory of expected utility.

Suppose I want to play a game. Let's say we are tossing a coin. If heads comes up, I win a dollar, and if tails comes up, I lose a dollar. Suppose further that I believe I know that the coin is asymmetrical and that the probability of getting heads (**p**) is greater than 50% – say 60% (0.6) – while the bookmaker assumes that the coin is totally symmetric. How much of my bankroll (T) should I optimally invest in this game?

On the use and misuse of theories and models in economics

A strict neoclassical utility-maximizing economist would suggest that my goal should be to maximize the expected value of my bankroll (wealth), and according to this view, I ought to bet my entire bankroll.

Does that sound rational? Most people would answer no to that question. The risk of losing is so high, that I already after few games played – the expected time until my first loss arises is 1/(1-p), which in this case is equal to 2.5 – with a high likelihood would be losing and thereby become bankrupt. The expected-value maximizing economist does not seem to have a particularly attractive approach.

So what's the alternative? One possibility is to apply the so-called Kelly criterion – after the American physicist and information theorist John L. Kelly, who in the article A New Interpretation of Information Rate [Kelly 1956] suggested this criterion for how to optimize the size of the bet – under which the optimum is to invest a specific fraction (x) of wealth (T) in each game. How do we arrive at this fraction?

When I win, I have ($1 + x$) times as much as before, and when I lose ($1 - x$) times as much. After n rounds, when I have won v times and lost $n - v$ times, my new bankroll

(W) is

$$(1) \quad W = (1 + x)^v (1 - x)^{n-v} T$$

[The bets used in these calculations are of the "quotient form" (Q), where you typically keep your bet money until the game is over, and a fortiori, in the win/lose expression it's not included that you get back what you bet when you win. If you prefer to think of odds calculations in the "decimal form" (D), where the bet money typically is considered lost when the game starts, you have to transform the calculations according to $Q = D - 1$.]

The bankroll increases multiplicatively – "compound interest" – and the long-term average growth rate for my wealth can then be easily calculated by taking the logarithms of (1), which gives

(2) $\log (W/ T) = v \log (1 + x) + (n - v) \log (1 - x)$.

If we divide both sides by n we get

(3) $[\log (W / T)] / n = [v \log (1 + x) + (n - v) \log (1 - x)] / n$

The left hand side now represents the *average* growth rate (g) in each game. On the right hand side the ratio v/n is equal to the percentage of bets that I won, and when n is large, this fraction will be close to p. Similarly, (n - v)/n is close to (1 - p). When the number of bets is large, the average growth rate is

(4) $g = p \log (1 + x) + (1 - p) \log (1 - x)$.

Now we can easily determine the value of x that maximizes g:

(5) $d [p \log (1 + x) + (1 - p) \log (1 - x)]/d x = p/(1 + x) - (1 - p)/(1 - x) =>$ $p/(1 + x) - (1 - p)/(1 - x) = 0 =>$

(6) $x = p - (1 - p)$

Since p is the probability that I will win, and (1 - p) is the probability that I will lose, the Kelly strategy says that to optimize the growth rate of your bankroll (wealth) you should invest a fraction of the bankroll equal to the difference of the likelihood that you will win or lose. In our example, this means that I have in each game to bet the fraction of x = 0.6 - (1 - 0.6) ≈ 0.2 – that is, 20% of my bankroll. Alternatively, we see that the Kelly criterion implies that we have to choose x so that $E[\log(1+x)]$ – which equals p log (1 + x) + (1 - p) log (1 - x) – is maximized.

The optimal average growth rate becomes

(7) 0.6 log (1.2) + 0.4 log (0.8) ≈ 0.02.

If I bet 20% of my wealth in tossing the coin, I will after 10 games on average have 1.02^{10} times more than when I started (≈ 1.22).

This game strategy will give us an outcome in the long run that is better than if we use a strategy building on the neoclassical economic theory of choice under uncertainty (risk) – expected value maximization. If we bet all our wealth in each game we will most likely lose our fortune, but because with low probability we will have a very large fortune, the expected value is still high. For a real-life player – for whom there is very little to benefit from this type of ensemble-average - it is more relevant to look at time-average of what he may be expected to win (in our game the averages are the same only if we assume that the player has a logarithmic utility function). What good does it do me if my tossing the coin maximizes an expected value when I might have gone bankrupt after four games played? If I try to maximize the expected value, the probability of bankruptcy soon gets close to one. Better then to invest 20% of my wealth in each game and maximize my long-term average wealth growth!

When applied to the neoclassical theory of expected utility, one thinks in terms of "parallel universe" and asks what is the expected return of an investment, calculated as an average over the "parallel universe"? In our coin toss example, it is as if one supposes that various "I" are tossing a coin and that the loss of many of them will be offset by the huge profits one of these "I" does. But this ensemble-average does not work for an individual, for whom a time-average better reflects the experience made in the "non-parallel universe" in which we live.

The Kelly criterion gives a more realistic answer, where one thinks in terms of the only universe we actually live in, and ask what is the expected return of an investment, calculated as an average over time.

Since we cannot go back in time – entropy and the "arrow of time" make this impossible – and the bankruptcy option is always at hand (extreme events and "black swans" are always possible) we have nothing to gain from thinking in terms of ensembles and "parallel universe".

Actual events follow a fixed pattern of time, where events are often linked in a multiplicative process (as e. g. investment returns with "compound interest") which is basically non-ergodic.

Instead of arbitrarily assuming that people have a certain type of utility function – as in the neoclassical theory – the Kelly criterion shows that we can obtain a less arbitrary and more accurate picture of real people's decisions and actions by basically assuming that time is irreversible. When the bankroll is gone, it's gone. The fact that in a parallel universe it could conceivably have been refilled, are of little comfort to those who live in the one and only possible world that we call the real world.

Our coin toss example can be applied to more traditional economic issues. If we think of an investor, we can basically describe his situation in terms of our coin toss. What fraction (x) of his assets (T) should an investor – who is about to make a large number of repeated investments – bet on his feeling that he can better evaluate an investment ($p = 0.6$) than the market ($p = 0.5$)? The greater the x, the greater is the leverage. But also – the greater is the risk. Since p is the probability that his investment valuation is correct and $(1 - p)$ is the probability that the market's valuation is correct, it means the Kelly criterion says he optimizes the rate of growth on his investments by investing a fraction of his assets that is equal to the difference in the probability that he will "win" or "lose". In our example this means that he at each investment opportunity is to invest the fraction of $x = 0.6 - (1 - 0.6)$, i.e. about 20% of his assets. The optimal average growth rate of investment is then about 2 % ($0.6 \log (1.2) + 0.4 \log (0.8)$).

Kelly's criterion shows that because we cannot go back in time, we should not take excessive risks. High leverage increases the risk of bankruptcy. This should also be a warning for the financial world, where the constant quest for greater and greater leverage – and risks – creates extensive and recurrent systemic crises. A more appropriate level of risk-taking is a necessary ingredient in a policy to come to curb excessive risk taking.

The works of people like Kelly and Kahneman show that expected utility theory is indeed transmogrifying truth.

On the use and misuse of theories and models in economics

Rational expectations – a fallacious foundation for macroeconomics in a non-ergodic world

In the wake of the latest financial crisis many people have come to wonder why economists never have been able to predict these manias, panics and crashes that intermittently haunt our economies. In responding to these warranted wonderings, some economists have maintained that it is a fundamental principle that there cannot be any reliable way of predicting a crisis.

This is a totally inadequate answer, and more or less trying to make an honour out of the inability of one's own science to give answers to just questions, is indeed proof of a rather arrogant attitude.

The main reason given for this view is what one of its staunchest defenders, David K. Levine (2012), calls "the uncertainty principle in economics" and the "theory of rational expectations":

> In simple language what rational expectations means is 'if people believe this forecast it will be true.' By contrast if a theory is not one of rational expectations it means 'if people believe this forecast it will not be true.' Obviously such a theory has limited usefulness. Or put differently: if there is a correct theory, eventually most people will believe it, so it must necessarily be rational expectations. Any other theory has the property that people must forever disbelieve the theory regardless of overwhelming evidence – for as soon as the theory is believed it is wrong.

> So does the crisis prove that rational expectations and rational behavior are bad assumptions for formulating economic policy? Perhaps we should turn to behavioral models of irrationality in understanding how to deal with the housing market crash or the Greek economic crisis? Such

an alternative would have us build on foundations of sand. It would have us create economic policies and institutions with the property that as soon as they were properly understood they would cease to function.

These are rather unsubstantiated allegations. To my knowledge, there are exceptionally few (if any) economists that really advocates constructing models based on irrational expectations. And very few of us are unaware of the effects that economic theory can have on the behaviour of economic actors. So – to put it bluntly – Levine fails to give a fair view of the state of play among contemporary economists on the issue of rational expectations. In this chapter, yours truly will attempt to substantiate that verdict.

Rational expectations – a concept with history

The concept of rational expectations was first developed by John Muth (1961) and later applied to macroeconomics by Robert Lucas (1972). In this way the concept of *uncertainty* as developed by Keynes (1921) and Knight (1921) was turned into a concept of quantifiable *risk* in the hands of neoclassical economics.

Muth (1961:316) framed his rational expectations hypothesis (REH) in terms of probability distributions:

> Expectations of firms (or, more generally, the subjective probability distribution of outcomes) tend to be distributed, for the same information set, about the prediction of the theory (or the "objective" probability distributions of outcomes).

But Muth (1961:317) was also very open with the non-descriptive character of his concept:

> The hypothesis of rational expectations *does not* assert that the scratch work of entrepreneurs resembles the

system of equations in any way; nor does it state that predictions of entrepreneurs are perfect or that their expectations are all the same.

To Muth its main usefulness was its generality and ability to be applicable to all sorts of situations irrespective of the concrete and contingent circumstances at hand. And while the concept was later picked up by New Classical Macroeconomics in the hands of people like Robert Lucas and Eugene Fama, most of us thought it was such a patently ridiculous idea, that we had problems with really taking it seriously.

It is noteworthy that Lucas (1972) did not give any further justifications for REH, but simply applied it to macroeconomics. In the hands of Lucas and Sargent it was used to argue that government could not really influence the behavior of economic agents in any systematic way. In the 1980s it became a dominant model assumption in New Classical Macroeconomics and has continued to be a standard assumption made in many neoclassical (macro)economic models – most notably in the fields of (real) business cycles and finance (being a cornerstone in the "efficient market hypothesis").

Keynes, genuine uncertainty, and ergodicity

REH basically says that people on the average hold expectations that will be fulfilled. This makes the economist's analysis enormously simplistic, since it means that the model used by the economist is the same as the one people use to make decisions and forecasts of the future.

This view is in obvious ways very different to the one we connect with John Maynard Keynes. According to Keynes (1937:113) we live in a world permeated by unmeasurable uncertainty – not quantifiable stochastic risk – which often force us to make decisions based on anything but rational expectations. Sometimes we "simply do not know".

Keynes would not have accepted Muth's view that expectations "tend to be distributed, for the same information set, about the prediction of the theory". Keynes, rather, thinks that we base our expectations on the confidence or "weight" we put on different events and alternatives. To Keynes expectations are a question of weighing probabilities by "degrees of belief," beliefs that have preciously little to do with the kind of stochastic probabilistic calculations made by the rational expectations agents modeled by Lucas *et consortes*.

Strictly seen, REH only applies to ergodic – stable and stationary stochastic – processes. Economies in the real world are nothing of the kind. In the real world, set in non-ergodic historical time, the future is to a large extent unknowable and uncertain. If the world was ruled by ergodic processes – a possibility utterly incompatible with the views of Keynes – people could perhaps have rational expectations, but no convincing arguments have ever been put forward, however, for this assumption being realistic.

REH holds the view that people, on average, have the same expectations. Keynes, on the other hand, argued convincingly that people often have *different* expectations and information, and that this constitutes the basic rational behind macroeconomic needs of coordination. This is something that is rather swept under the rug by the extreme simple- mindedness of assuming rational expectations in representative actors models, which is so in vogue in New Classical Economics. Indeed if all actors are alike, why do they transact? Who do they transact with? The very reason for markets and exchange seems to slip away with the sister assumptions of representative actors and rational expectations.

Mathematical tractability is not enough

It is hard to escape the conclusion that it is an enormous waste of intellectual power to build these kinds of models based on next to useless theories. Their marginal utility have long since passed over into the negative. That people are still more or less mindlessly doing this is a sign of some kind of – not so little – intellectual hubris.

It would be far better to admit that we "simply do not know" about lots of different things, and that we should try to do as good as possible given this, rather than looking the other way and pretend that we are all-knowing rational calculators.

Models based on REH impute beliefs to the agents that are not based on any real informational considerations, but simply *stipulated* to make the models mathematically- statistically tractable. Of course you can make assumptions based on tractability, but then you do also have to take into account the necessary trade-off in terms of the ability to make relevant and valid statements on the intended target system. Mathematical tractability cannot be the ultimate arbiter in science when it comes to modeling real world target systems. Of course, one could perhaps accept REH if it had produced lots of verified predictions and good explanations. But it has done nothing of the kind. Therefore the burden of proof is on those who still want to use models built on ridiculously unreal assumptions – models devoid of obvious empirical interest.

In reality REH is a rather harmful modeling assumption, since it contributes to perpetuating the ongoing transformation of economics into a kind of science-fiction-economics. If economics is to guide us, help us make forecasts, explain or better understand real world phenomena, it is in fact next to worthless.

Learning and information

REH presupposes – basically for reasons of consistency – that agents have complete knowledge of *all* of the relevant probability distribution functions. And when trying to incorporate learning in these models – to take the heat off some of the criticism launched against it up to date – it is always a very restricted kind of learning that is considered (cf. Evans & Honkapohja, 2001). A learning where truly unanticipated, surprising, new things never take place, but only a rather mechanical updating – increasing the precision of already existing information sets – of existing probability functions.

Nothing really new happens in these ergodic models, where the statistical representation of learning and information is nothing more than a caricature of what takes place in the real world target system. This follows from taking for granted that people's decisions can be portrayed as based on an existing probability distribution, which by definition implies the knowledge of every possible event – otherwise it is, in a strict mathematical-statistical sense, not really a probability distribution – that can be thought of as taking place.

But in the real world it is – as shown again and again by behavioural and experimental economics – common to mistake a conditional distribution for a probability distribution. These are mistakes that are *impossible* to make in the kinds of economic analysis that are built on REH. On average REH agents are always correct. But truly new information will not only reduce the estimation error but actually change the entire estimation and hence possibly the decisions made. To be truly new, information has to be unexpected. If not, it would simply be inferred from the already existing information set.

In REH models new information is typically presented as something only reducing the variance of the parameter estimated. But if new information means truly new information it actually could increase our uncertainty and variance (information set (A, B) => (A, B, C)). Truly new information gives birth to new probabilities, revised plans and decisions – something the REH cannot account for with its finite sampling representation of incomplete information.

In the world of REH, learning is like being better and better at reciting the complete works of Shakespeare by heart – or at hitting bull's eye when playing darts. It presupposes that we have a complete list of the possible states of the world and that by definition mistakes are non-systematic (which, strictly seen, follows from the assumption of "subjective" probability distributions being equal to the "objective" probability distribution). This is a rather uninteresting and trivial kind of learning. It is a closed world learning, synonymous to improving one's adaptation to a world which is fundamentally unchanging. But in real, open world situations, learning is more often about adapting and trying to cope with genuinely new phenomena.

REH presumes consistent behaviour, where expectations do not display any persistent errors. In the world of REH we are always, on average, hitting the bull's eye. In the more realistic, open systems view, there is always the possibility (danger) of making mistakes that may turn out to be systematic. It is presumably one of the main reasons why we put so much emphasis on learning in our modern knowledge societies.

On risk, uncertainty and probability distributions

REH assumes that the expectations based on "objective" probabilities are the same as the "subjective" probabilities that agents themselves form on uncertain events. It treats risk and uncertainty as equivalent entities.

But in the real world, it is not possible to just *assume* that probability distributions are the right way to characterize, understand or explain acts and decisions made under uncertainty. When we "simply do not know," when we "haven't got a clue," when genuine uncertainty prevails – REH simply will not do. In those circumstances it is not a useful assumption. The reason is that under those circumstances the future is not like the past, and henceforth, we cannot use the same probability distribution – if it at all exists – to describe both the past and future.

There simply is no guarantee that probabilities at time x are the same as those at time x+i. So when REH assumes that the parameter values on average are the same for the future and the past, one is – as Roman Frydman and Michael Goldberg (2007) forcefully argue – not really talking about uncertainty, but rather knowledge. But this implies that what we observe are realizations of pure stochastic processes, something – if we really want to maintain this view – we have to *argue* for.

In physics it may possibly not be straining credulity too much to model processes as ergodic – where time and history do not really matter – but in social and historical sciences it is obviously ridiculous. If societies and economies were ergodic worlds, why do econometricians fervently discuss things such as structural breaks and regime shifts? That they do is an indication of the unrealisticness of treating open systems as analyzable with ergodic concepts.

The future is not reducible to a known set of prospects. It is not like sitting at the roulette table and calculating what the future outcomes of spinning the wheel will be. A more realistic foundation for economics has to encompass both ergodic and non-ergodic processes, both risk and genuine uncertainty. Reading advocates of REH one comes to think of Robert Clower's (1989:23) apt remark that:

> much economics is so far removed from anything that remotely resembles the real world that it's often difficult for economists to take their own subject seriously.

Where do probabilities come from in REH?

In REH models, events and observations are as a rule interpreted as random variables, as if generated by an underlying probability density function, and *a fortiori* – since probability density functions are only definable in a probability context – consistent with a probability. When attempting to convince us of the necessity of founding empirical economic analysis on probability models, advocates of REH actually force us to (implicitly) interpret events as random variables generated by an underlying probability density function. This is at odds with reality. Randomness obviously is a fact of the real world. Probability, on the other hand, attaches to the world via intellectually constructed models, and is only a fact of a probability generating machine or a well-constructed experimental arrangement or "chance set-up". Just as there is no such thing as a "free lunch", there is no such thing as a "free probability". To be able at all to talk about probabilities, you have to specify a model. If there is no chance set-up or model that generates the probabilistic outcomes or events – in statistics one refers to any process where you observe or measure as an *experiment* (rolling a die) and the results obtained as the *outcomes* or *events* (number of points rolled with the die, being e. g. 3 or 5) of the experiment –there strictly seen is no event at all.

Probability is a relational element. It always must come with a specification of the model from which it is calculated. And then to be of any empirical scientific value it has to be *shown* to coincide with (or at least converge to) real data generating processes or structures – something seldom or never done!

And this is the basic problem with economic data. If you have a fair roulette-wheel, you can arguably specify probabilities and probability density distributions. But how do you conceive of the analogous – to speak with science philosopher Nancy Cartwright (1999) – "nomological machines" for prices, gross domestic product, income distribution, etc.? Only by a leap of faith. And that does not suffice. You have to come up with some really good arguments if you want to persuade people into believing in the existence of socioeconomic structures that generate data with characteristics conceivable as stochastic events portrayed by probabilistic density distributions.

From a realistic point of view we have to admit that the socio-economic states of nature that we talk of in most social sciences – and certainly in economics – are not amenable to analysis as probabilities, simply because in the real world open systems that social sciences (including economics) analyze, there are, strictly seen, no probabilities to be had!

The processes that generate socio-economic data in the real world cannot *simpliciter* be assumed to always be adequately captured by a probability measure. And, so, it cannot convincingly be maintained, as in REH, that it should be mandatory to treat observations and data – whether cross-section, time series or panel data – as events generated by some probability model. The important activities of most economic agents do not usually include throwing dice or spinning roulette-wheels. Data generating processes – at least outside of nomological machines like dice and roulette-wheels – are not self-evidently best modeled with probability measures.

If we agree on this, we also have to admit that theories like REH, lacks a sound justification. I would even go further and argue that there is no justifiable rationale at all for this belief that all economically relevant data can be adequately captured by a probability measure. In most real world contexts one has to *argue* one's case. And that is obviously something almost never done by practitioners of REH and its probabilistically based econometric analyses.

The conception of randomness in REH

Deep down there is also a problem with the conception of randomness in REH models. In REH models probability is often (implicitly) defined with the help of independent trials – two events are said to be *independent* if the occurrence or nonoccurrence of either one has no effect on the probability of the occurrence of the other – as drawing cards from a deck, picking balls from an urn, spinning a roulette wheel or tossing coins – trials which are only definable if somehow set in a probabilistic context.

But if we pick a sequence of prices – say 2, 4, 3, 8, 5, 6 – that we want to use in an econometric regression analysis, how do we know the sequence of prices is random and a *fortiori* being able to treat it as generated by an underlying probability density function? How can we argue that the sequence is a sequence of probabilistically independent random prices? And are they really random in the sense that is most often applied in REH models (where X is called a *random variable* only if there is a sample space S with a probability measure and X is a real-valued function over the elements of S)?

Bypassing the scientific challenge of going from describable randomness to calculable probability by simply assuming it, is of course not an acceptable procedure. Since a probability density function is a "Gedanken" object that does not exist in a natural sense, it has to come with an export license to our real target system if it is to be considered usable. Among those who at least honestly try to face the problem – the usual procedure is to refer to some artificial mechanism operating in some "games of chance" of the kind mentioned above and which generates the sequence. But then we still have to show that the real sequence somehow coincides with the ideal sequence that defines independence and randomness within our nomological machine, our probabilistic model.

So why should we define randomness with probability? If we do, we have to accept that to speak of randomness we also have to presuppose the existence of nomological probability machines, since probabilities cannot be spoken of – and actually, to be strict, do not at all exist - without specifying such system-contexts (how many sides do the dice have, are the cards unmarked, etc.).

If we do adhere to the REH paradigm we also have to assume that all noise in our data is probabilistic and that errors are well-behaving, something that is hard to justifiably argue for as a real phenomena, and not just an operationally and pragmatically tractable assumption. Accepting the usual REH domain of probability theory and sample space of infinite populations – just as Fisher's (1922:311) "hypothetical infinite population, of which the actual data are regarded as constituting a random sample", von Mises' "collective" or Gibbs' "ensemble" – also implies that judgments are made on the basis of observations that are actually never made!

Infinitely repeated trials or samplings never take place in the real world. So that cannot be a sound inductive basis for a science with aspirations of explaining real world socio-economic processes, structures or events. It's not tenable. As David Salsburg (2001:146) notes on probability theory:

> [W]e assume there is an abstract space of elementary things called 'events' ... If a measure on the abstract space of events fulfills certain axioms, then it is a probability. To use probability in real life, we have to identify this space of events and do so with sufficient specificity to allow us to actually calculate probability measurements on that space ... Unless we can identify [this] abstract space, the probability statements that emerge from statistical analyses will have many different and sometimes contrary meanings.

On the use and misuse of theories and models in economics

Just as e. g. Keynes (1921) and Georgescu-Roegen (1971), Salsburg (2001:301f) is very critical of the way social scientists – including economists and econometricians – uncritically and *without arguments* have come to simply assume that one can apply probability distributions from statistical theory on their own area of research:

> Probability is a measure of sets in an abstract space of events. All the mathematical properties of probability can be derived from this definition. When we wish to apply probability to real life, we need to identify that abstract space of events for the particular problem at hand... It is not well established when statistical methods are used for observational studies... If we cannot identify the space of events that generate the probabilities being calculated, then one model is no more valid than another... As statistical models are used more and more for observational studies to assist in social decisions by government and advocacy groups, this fundamental failure to be able to derive probabilities without ambiguity will cast doubt on the usefulness of these methods.

This importantly also means that if advocates of REH cannot show that data satisfies *all* the conditions of the probabilistic nomological machine – including e. g. the distribution of the deviations corresponding to a normal curve – then the statistical inferences used lack sound foundations!

Of course one could treat our observational or experimental data as random samples from real populations. I have no problem with that. But probabilistic econometrics does not content itself with that kind of populations. Instead it creates imaginary populations of "parallel universe" and assumes that our data are random samples from that kind of populations. But this is actually nothing but hand-waving! And it is inadequate for real science. As eminent mathematical statistician David Freedman (2009:27) writes:

> With this approach, the investigator does not explicitly define a population that could in principle be studied, with

unlimited resources of time and money. The investigator merely *assumes* that such a population exists in some ill-defined sense. And there is a further assumption, that the data set being analyzed can be treated *as if* it were based on a random sample from the assumed population. These are convenient fictions... Nevertheless, reliance on imaginary populations is widespread. Indeed regression models are commonly used to analyze convenience samples... The rhetoric of imaginary populations is seductive because it seems to free the investigator from the necessity of understanding how data were generated.

Where is the evidence?

Instead of assuming REH to be right, one ought to confront the hypothesis with the available evidence. It is not enough to construct models. Anyone can construct models. To be seriously interesting, a model has to come with an aim, it has to have an intended use. If the intention of REH is to help us explain real economies, it has to be evaluated from that perspective. A model or hypothesis without a specific applicability does not really deserve our interest.

To say, as Prescott (1977:30), that:

> one can only test if some theory, whether it incorporates rational expectations or, for that matter, irrational expectations, is or is not *consistent* with observations

is not enough. Without strong evidence, all kinds of absurd claims and nonsense may pretend to be science. When it comes to rationality postulates, we have to demand more of a justification than this rather watered-down version of "anything goes". Proposing REH, one also has to *support* its underlying assumptions. None is given, which makes it rather puzzling how REH has become the standard modeling assumption made in much of modern macroeconomics. Perhaps the reason is, as Paul

Krugman (2009) has it, that economists often mistake "beauty, clad in impressive looking mathematics, for truth". But I think Prescott's view is also the reason why REH economists are not particularly interested in empirical examinations of how real choices and decisions are made in real economies. In the hands of Lucas *et consortes*, REH has been transformed from being an – in principle – testable *hypothesis* to being an irrefutable *proposition*.

Rational expectations, the future, and the end of history

REH basically assumes that all learning has already taken place. This is extremely difficult to vision in reality, because that means that history has come to an end. When did that happen? It is indeed a remarkable assumption, since in our daily life, most of us experience a continuing learning. It may be a tractable assumption, yes. But helpful to understand real world economies? No. REH builds on Savage's (1954) "sure thing principle", according to which people never make systematic mistakes. They may "tremble" now and then, but on average, they always make the right – the rational – decision. That kind of models is not useful "as-if" representations of real world target systems.

In REH agents know all possible outcomes. In reality, many of those outcomes are yet to be originated. The future is not about known probability distributions. It is not about picking the right ball from an urn. It is about new possibilities. It is about inventing new balls and new urns to put them in. If so, even if we learn, uncertainty does not go away. As G. L. S. Shackle (1972:102) argued, the future "waits, not for its contents to be discovered, but for that content to be originated".

As shown already by Davidson (1983) REH implies – by the implicit ergodicity assumption – that relevant distributions have to be *time independent*. But this amounts to assuming that an economy is like a closed system with known stochastic probability distributions for all different events. In reality it is straining one's beliefs to try to represent economies as outcomes of stochastic processes. An existing economy is a single realization *tout court*, and hardly conceivable as one realization out of an

126

ensemble of economy-worlds, since an economy can hardly be conceived as being completely replicated over time.

The arrow of time and the difference between time averages and ensemble averages

In REH we are never disappointed in any other way than as when we lose at the roulette wheels, since "averages of expectations are accurate" (Muth 1961:316). But real life is not an urn or a roulette wheel, so REH is a vastly misleading analogy of real world situations. It is not even useful for non-crucial and non-important decisions that are possible to replicate perfectly (a throw of dices, a spin of the roulette wheel etc.).

Time is what prevents everything from happening at once. To simply assume that economic processes are ergodic – a fortiori in any relevant sense timeless – and concentrate on ensemble averages is not a sensible way for dealing with the kind of genuine uncertainty that permeates open systems such as economies.

Since ergodicity and the all-important difference between time averages and ensemble averages are somewhat difficult concepts, let me just try to explain the meaning of these concepts by means of a couple of simple examples. Let's say you're offered a gamble where on a roll of a fair die you will get €10 billion if you roll a six, and pay me €1 billion if you roll any other number. Would you accept the gamble?

If you're a neoclassical economist you probably would, because that's what you're taught to be the only thing consistent with being rational. You would arrest the arrow of time by imagining six different "parallel universes" where the independent outcomes are the numbers from one to six, and then weight them using their stochastic probability distribution.

Calculating the expected value of the gamble – the ensemble average – by averaging on all these weighted outcomes you would actually be an odd person if you didn't take the gamble (the expected value of the gamble being 5/6*€0 + 1/6*€10 billion = €1.67 billion).

If you're not a neoclassical economist you would probably trust your common sense and decline the offer, knowing that a large risk of bankrupting one's economy is not a very rosy perspective for the future. Since you can't really arrest or reverse the arrow of time, you know that once you have lost the €1 billion, it's all over. The large likelihood that you go bust weights heavier than the 17 % chance of you becoming enormously rich. By computing the time average – imagining one real universe where the six different but dependent outcomes occur consecutively – we would soon be aware of our assets disappearing, and *a fortiori* that it would be irrational to accept the gamble. [From a mathematical point of view you can somewhat non-rigorously describe the difference between ensemble averages and time averages as a difference between arithmetic averages and geometric averages. Tossing a fair coin and gaining 20 % on the stake (S) if winning (heads) and having to pay 20 % on the stake (S) if loosing (tails), the arithmetic average of the return on the stake, assuming the outcomes of the coin-toss being independent, would be [(0.5*1.2S + 0.5*0.8S) - S)/S] = 0 %. If considering the two outcomes of the toss not being independent, the relevant time average would be a geometric average return of square-root [(1.2S *0.8S)] /S - 1= - 2 %.]

Why is the difference between ensemble and time averages of such importance in economics? Well, basically, because when – as in REH – assuming the processes to be ergodic, ensemble and time averages are identical. [Assume we have a market with an asset priced at €100. Then imagine the price first goes up by 50 % and then later falls by 50 %. The ensemble average for this asset would be €100 – because we here envision two parallel universes (markets) where the asset price falls in one universe (market) with 50 % to €50, and in another universe (market) it goes up with 50 % to €150, giving an average of 100€ ((150 + 50)/2). The time average for this asset would be 75 € – because we here envision one universe (market) where the asset price first rises by 50 % to €150, and then falls by 50 % to €75 (0.5*150).]

Rational expectations

From the ensemble perspective nothing, on average, happens. From the time perspective lots of things, really, on average, happen. Assuming ergodicity there would have been no difference at all. When applied to the neoclassical theory of expected utility – which usually comes with REH models – one thinks in terms of "parallel universe" and ask what is the expected return of an investment, calculated as an average over the "parallel universe"? In our coin-tossing example, it is as if one supposes that various "I" is tossing a coin and that the loss of many of them will be offset by the huge profits one of these "I" does. But this ensemble average does not work for an individual, for whom a time average better reflects the experience made in the "non-parallel universe" in which we live.

Time averages gives a more realistic answer, where one thinks in terms of the only universe we actually live in, and ask what is the expected return of an investment, calculated as an average over time. Since we cannot go back in time – entropy and the arrow of time make this impossible – and the bankruptcy option is always at hand (extreme events and "black swans" are always possible) we have nothing to gain from – as in REH models – thinking in terms of ensembles.

Actual events follow a fixed pattern of time, where events are often linked in a multiplicative process (as e. g. investment returns with "compound interest") that is basically non-ergodic.

Instead of arbitrarily assuming that people have a certain type of utility function – as in the neoclassical theory – time average considerations show that we can obtain a less arbitrary and more accurate picture of real people's decisions and actions by basically assuming that time is irreversible. When our assets are gone, they are gone. The fact that in a parallel universe it could conceivably have been refilled, is of little comfort to those who live in the one and only possible world that we call the real world.

REH and modeling aspirations of Nirvana

REH comes from the belief that to be scientific, economics has to be able to model individuals and markets in a stochastic-deterministic way. It's like treating individuals and markets as the celestial bodies studied by astronomers with the help of gravitational laws. But – individuals, markets and entire economies are not planets moving in predetermined orbits in the sky.

To deliver, REH has to constrain expectations on the individual and the aggregate level to actually be the same. If revisions of expectations take place in the REH models, they typically have to take place in a known and pre-specified precise way. This squares badly with what we know to be true in the real world, where fully specified trajectories of future expectations revisions are non-existent.

Most REH models are time-invariant and so give no room for any changes in expectations and their revisions. The only imperfection of knowledge they admit is included in the error terms – error terms that are assumed to be additive and have a given and known frequency distribution, so that the REH models can still fully pre-specify the future even when incorporating these stochastic variables into the models.

In the real world there are many different expectations and these cannot be aggregated in REH models without giving rise to inconsistency (acknowledged by Lucas (1995:225) himself). This is one of the main reasons for REH models being modeled as representative actors models. But this is far from being a harmless approximation to reality (cf. Syll (2010)). Even the smallest differences of expectations between agents would make REH models inconsistent, so when they still show up they have to be considered "irrational".

It is not possible to adequately represent individuals and markets as having one single overarching probability distribution. Accepting that, does not imply – as advocates of REH seem to think – that we have to end all theoretical endeavours and assume that all agents always act totally irrationally and only are analyzable within behavioural economics.

Far from it – it means we acknowledge diversity and imperfection, and that economic theory has to be able to incorporate these empirical facts in its models. Incompatibility between actual behaviour and REH behaviour is not a symptom of "irrationality". It rather shows the futility of trying to represent real world target systems with models flagrantly at odds with reality.

Conclusion

The financial crisis of 2007-08 hit most laymen and economists with surprise. What was it that went wrong with mainstream neoclassical macroeconomic models, since they obviously did not foresee the collapse or even make it conceivable?

As I have tried to show in this book, one important reason ultimately goes back to how these models handle data. In REH-based modern neoclassical macroeconomics – Dynamic Stochastic General Equilibrium (DSGE), New Synthesis, New Classical, "New Keynesian" – variables are treated as if drawn from a known "data-generating process" that unfolds over time and on which one therefore have access to heaps of historical time-series. If one does not assume the "data-generating process" to be known – if there is no "true" model – the whole edifice collapses.

Building on REH, modern macroeconomics obviously did not anticipate the enormity of the problems that unregulated "efficient" financial markets created. Why? Because it builds on the myth of us knowing the "data-generating process" and that we can describe the variables of our evolving economies as drawn from an urn containing stochastic probability functions with known means and variances.

This is like saying that you are going on a holiday-trip and that you know that the chance the weather being sunny is at least 30%, and that this is enough for you to decide on bringing along your sunglasses or not. You are supposed to be able to calculate the expected utility based on the given probability of sunny weather and make a simple decision of either-or. Uncertainty is reduced to risk. But this is not always possible. Often we "simply do not know". According to one model the chance of sunny weather is perhaps somewhere around 10 % and according to another – equally good – model the chance is perhaps somewhere around 40 %. We cannot put exact numbers on these assessments. We cannot calculate means and variances. There are no given probability distributions that we can appeal to.

In the end this is what it all boils down to. We all know that many activities, relations, processes and events are of the Keynesian uncertainty type. The data do not – as REH models assume – unequivocally single out one decision as the only "rational" one. Neither the economist, nor the deciding individual, can fully pre-specify how people will decide when facing uncertainties and ambiguities that are ontological facts of the way the world works.

Some macroeconomists, however, still want to be able to use their hammer. So they decide to pretend that the world looks like a nail, and pretend that uncertainty can be reduced to risk. So they construct their mathematical models on that assumption. The result: financial crises and economic havoc.

How much better – how much bigger chance that we do not lull us into the comforting thought that we know everything and that everything is measurable and we have everything under control – if instead we would just admit that we often "simply do not know," and that we have to live with that uncertainty as well as it goes. Fooling people into believing that one can cope with an unknown economic future in a way similar to playing at the roulette wheels, is a sure recipe for only one thing – economic catastrophe. The *unknown knowns* – the things we fool ourselves to believe we know – often have more dangerous repercussions than the "Black Swans" of Knightian unknown unknowns, something quantitative risk management – based on the hypotheses of market efficiency and rational expectations – has given ample evidence of during the latest financial crisis.

Defenders of REH, like David K. Levine (2012), maintains that "the only robust policies and institutions – ones that we may hope to withstand the test of time – are those based on rational expectations – those that once understood will continue to function." As argued in this book, there is really no support for this conviction at all. On the contrary – if we want to have anything of interest to say on real economies, financial crisis and the decisions and choices real people make, it is high time to place the rational expectations hypothesis where it belongs – in the dustbin of history.

Interestingly enough, the main developer of REH himself, Robert Lucas – in an interview with Kevin Hoover (2013a) – has himself had some second-thoughts on the validity of REH:

> Kevin Hoover: The Great Recession and the recent financial crisis have been widely viewed in both popular and professional commentary as a challenge to rational expectations and to efficient markets... I'm asking you whether you accept any of the blame... there's been a lot of talk about whether rational expectations and the efficient-markets hypotheses is where we should locate the analytical problems that made us blind.

> Robert Lucas: You know, people had no trouble having financial meltdowns in their economies before all this stuff we've been talking about came on board. We didn't help, though; there's no question about that. We may have focused attention on the wrong things, I don't know.

We're looking forward to see some more future second-thoughts on the subject from other advocates of REH as well. Better late than never.

On the use and misuse of theories and models in economics

Neoliberalism and neoclassical economics

Neoliberalism as a political doctrine and as an economic theory have always been closely connected. To begin with, both take their point of departure from John Locke's formulation of a political philosophy from a theory of natural rights. If a person has a right to himself, he has also, according to Locke, a right to the property that follows from his labour, given that it does not impinge on the rights of others. Even if it is easy for a neo-classical economist, with his view of man as fundamentally a *homo oeconomicus*, to get into neo-liberal positions, and even if economic theory has made itself especially noticeable lately, one cannot restrict neo-liberalism to being a narrow economic doctrine.

In principle, it may be said two kinds of neo-liberalism exist today. First, we have a libertarian tradition – from Aristoteles and John Locke to Ayn Rand, Eric Mack, Loren Lomasky, Tibor Machan, Jan Narveson, Murray Rothbard, David Friedman and Robert Nozick – which takes, as its point of departure, a natural rights based-rights-perspective and has a philosophical rather than economic-theoretical starting-point. Secondly we have an economistic tradition – from Adam Smith and John Stuart Mill to Ludwig von Mises, Friedrich von Hayek, Milton Friedman and James Buchanan – that primarily justifies free markets and capitalism with efficiency arguments. To these, freedom has mostly an instrumental value and is wanted only in so far as it leads to the wished for consequences, that are realised when markets are left to govern themselves with as little as possible government involvement.

Amartya Sen has, for many decades, directed severe criticism against both these kinds of neo-liberalism. The aim of this chapter is to try to position this critique of neo-liberalism. To make this as simple and accessible as possible I will analyse the two neoliberal traditions below and present Sen's incisive views along the way.

On the use and misuse of theories and models in economics

The Libertarian Tradition

Nozick's *Anarchy, State, and Utopia* is undoubtedly the most central work in the modern libertarian tradition. I will begin my presentation by an analysis of some of the bearing ideas in his seminal work.

Nozick's theory is based on what he perceives to be historically legitimately attained rights ("entitlements"). According to this a distribution's fairness should be evaluated from how it originated and not from its consequences, making it fair if it has come about in the right way, i.e. without violating anyone's rights.

Why do we have to accept the special standing of the rights? Is it really right to treat rights as inviolable independently of consequences? In real life many large reallocations occur (e. g. via the market) of "life-possibilities" without violating legal rights. Some become unemployed, or have to leave their homes or starve. Why do we have to accept this, and in what way is it just or right? Nozick has to take a firm stand on these questions since his consequence-independent view on rights would otherwise collapse totally. Procedural arguments do not allow exceptions. Rights and freedoms are of course important, and have to be considered when, for example, the consequences of a distribution are evaluated. But they should not be considered absolute and unconditional restrictions. Even the institutions that Nozick tries to legitimise with his theory – especially the free market – have to be considered from the point of view of their consequences. To judge the value of the market we have to understand fundamental social values such as well-being, freedom and justice. As Amartya Sen [2000:143] has it: "The far-reaching powers of the market mechanism have to be supplemented by the creation of basic social equity and justice."

Nozick is critical of the view that many rights-theoreticians have, namely that what has to be divided is a given cake, and that the "cake-dividing problem" can be treated independently of *who* has produced the cake and *how*. According to Nozick the problem cannot be divided into two independent parts, since the cake has been produced by individuals and these have rights attached to the cake.

136

The point of departure for Nozick's rights-theory is that every individual has rights to himself and that the individual in this regard is unique. Freedom and property-rights also follow from these founding rights. That the list of rights is no longer than this, is not by chance. Nozick cannot extend the rights to include e.g. welfare without making his theory inconsistent. But Nozick never gives, amazingly enough, any grounds for his principle of self-ownership. He only refers to Locke as an authority and abstains from anything that is even faintly reminiscent of a satisfactory justification.

The derived rights originate [Nozick 1974:174] through "someone's mixing his labor" with an "unowned object" and follow from the fact that "one owns one's labor".

But why should an individual's property-right be for the *whole* value of the object that his work is mixed with? Why is the property-right not only for the part of the extra value that one's work has added to the object? Nozick gives no convincing answers, but only refers again to Locke's proviso that there "be enough and as good left in common for others". Nozick interprets this to mean that if appropriation of a non-owned object worsens the situation of others, the proviso is violated.

Compared to Locke's formulation, Nozick's is less severe. Where Locke means that there has to be "enough and as good" left to others, Nozick is satisfied by stipulating that the appropriation does not worsen the situation for others compared to continued use of the object. And even if the proviso was violated, Nozick [1974:178] means that it could be compensated "so that their situation is not thereby worsened".

This implies that Nozick's proviso can be satisfied even when an individual is worse off because of an appropriation, given that he can be sufficiently rewarded. But how do we know that the compensation is sufficient?

There is a fundamental weakness in the whole of Nozick's argumentation in the defence of the private property-right and its inviolability. If property is appropriated without *physical* violence it is according to the libertarian demands, unforced. But this cannot be the starting point of the reasoning but rather a conclusion. This is not the case with Nozick. On the whole his definition of coercion is strange. If a criminal righteously is put into jail, he is, in Nozick's view, not forced to stay in prison. Such a juggling with concepts confuses more than it enlightens. Nozick's "moralized" definition of coercion (A is only forced to do x when he is exposed to *illegitimate* force) and the argument built on it, is doubtful. To say that we are exposed to force only when it is illegitimate has counterintuitive consequences. When Nozick discusses the Lockean proviso it never occurs to him that one person's appropriation can restrict another person's liberty by giving the property-owner larger possibilities of dictating the other person's life- and working-conditions. Nozick asserts that property-rights do not restrict freedom in his theory since they are valid. But given the special position of liberty in his theory, the question of whether the entitlements infringe on liberty has to be answered before it can be said that they are valid. The coercion that exists in the capitalistic relation is a structural coercion that emanates out of a group's exclusive ownership and control over resources. How these resources came to belong to this group is less relevant from the point of view of justice.

According to Nozick all of society's attempts to influence welfare infringe on liberty. But do they really? At university, for example, teaching positions are held by different persons according to certain criteria (patterns) – deserts, academic merits, etc. That we do not allow the holders of these positions to testament away their lectureships or professorships is difficult to perceive as a restriction of their freedom. To show that the patterns alter the freedom, Nozick first has to show that we have the right to carry out exactly whatever transfers we want to. But is liberty then really fundamental any longer? This is symptomatic for the whole of Nozick's project, i.e. he wants to unite property rights and liberty. These are, however, difficult to unite and ultimately liberty has to be given up.

Sen's critique of Nozick

Sen has criticized Nozick's rights-based ethics for giving – like other duty-based ethical systems – a far too simple and one-dimensional solution to complex social and moral problems. In *Inequality Reexamined* Sen [1992:21] writes that Nozick's approach is a lucid and elegant example of the strategy of "justifying inequality through equality".

In particular, Sen contends that Nozick is not able to give a trustworthy answer on the issue of handling situations where rights and freedoms are dependent on each other. The ethics of duty must be complemented with the type of consequence-valuations that are used within economics to give a more correct formulation of rights and freedom. With examples taken from e.g. his research on poverty and famines, Sen has tried to show that Nozick's consequence-independent approach is misleading. Hunger and famines can also emerge in societies whose systems of rights may live up to the conditions set out in Nozick's theory. If the possible consequences of a distribution of rights are hunger and famines, these terrible consequences should lead to a questioning of the rights-system's moral justification. Rules of property rights have no self-evident superior priority when we confront issues of life and death. There are no absolute rights, because what is often put into question is precisely the legitimacy of those rights.

Libertarianism as liberty

Many neo-liberals (c.f. Gauthier [1986]) today feel that Nozick's theory does not have the power to convince. Instead they mean that neo-liberalism should be conceived as a theory of mutual utility or as a theory of liberty.

Especially the latter has become common during the last ten years and argues that the unhampered market-society implies greater freedom than any other existing alternative. However, the theory is, as Sen and other critics have shown, founded on a serious error. It is not abstract freedom that it is all about, but rather the freedoms and interests that are important and ought to be furthered. There is a difference between restricting our freedom to drive a vehicle at high speed in highly populated areas and restricting our freedom of speech. The latter freedom is simply so much more essential for making it possible for us to realise our "life-possibilities" and our fundamental life-projects.

Liberty-oriented libertarianism attacks the view that we as citizens should be entitled to other rights than those of speech, religion and property. Social rights – the right to medical attention, education, work and welfare – are not considered "real" human rights. Trying to assert anything else is said only to lead to a dangerous enlargement of state supremacy and devaluation of the status of rights.

Libertarianism takes its point of departure from a formulation of a theory of natural rights, where the rights are looked upon as sacred. Why we have to accept these rights' exceptional status is, however, not obvious. Rights and freedom make possible the realisation of our life-plans and ideas of the good life. But they cannot – as often pointed out by Amartya Sen – be considered absolute and inviolable restrictions.

Rights and freedoms are of course connected to each other. That is the reason why libertarians want to restrict the meaning of the concept of freedom to only negative freedom – the absence of coercion. Not any kind of coercion, but only when *persons* exercise coercion is freedom held to be restricted. If social structures and property rights deny people access to food, education and safety, no one's freedom is said to be restricted. That lack of property does not only prevent the property-less' self-determination, but also makes him an instrument to attaining others' goals never enters the libertarian's mind. Nor does the fact that some people's property rights restrict others' freedom.

To libertarians every re-distribution of welfare that ignores property rights is indefensible. But why should property rights be put above our rights to medical attention, education and health? To secure the possibilities of a decent life may demand redistribution, and meaningful freedom presupposes that we can develop our capabilities and take part in the welfare. Freedom has to do with more than property.

Amartya Sen has much to say about the libertarian idea of properties and the wonders of market economy. He has at various times scrutinised the libertarian theories and their rights or entitlement-based ethics and criticised them for giving a too simple and one-dimensional solution to complex social moral problems. Sen especially criticises the libertarians for not giving credible answers on how to handle situations where rights and liberty are mutually dependent on each other. Their deontological ethics must be supplemented with consequence-evaluations to enable them to give an adequate formulation of rights and freedoms.

Sen [1987:72] gives an example in *On Ethics & Economics*: "If person A is violating in a serious way some right of B, e.g. beating him up badly, does person C have a duty to help prevent this? Further would C be justified in some minor violation of some other right of person D to help prevent the more important violation of B's rights by strong-armed A? Could C, for example, take without permission – let us say by force – a car belonging to D who is not willing to lend it to C, to rush to the spot to rescue B from being beaten up by A."

Not according to Nozick's entitlement system (and other libertarian versions as well) since C is not obliged to help B and is obliged not to violate the rights of D. Omitting to act in such a situation does not violate anyone's freedom according to libertarians. With such a view one can argue like Gauthier [1986:218]: "The rich man may feast on caviar and champagne, while the poor woman starves at his gate. And she may not even take the crumbs from his table, if that would deprive him of his pleasure in feeding them to his birds." Such a "liberal liberty- and rights-system" is, however, hardly credible.

With many examples from his research on poverty and famines, Sen has tried to show that the consequence-independent view of the libertarians is basically misleading. Famine and starvation can appear even in a society whose rights-system at large would correspond to the libertarian theory. If the consequences of the distribution of rights are famine and starvation, these horrible consequences should lead to a questioning of the moral justification of the rights-system. As noticed above, rights of freedom and rules of property-rights have no self-evident overarching priority when we face issues of life and death. To Sen, it is self-evident that we should not make a fetish out of freedom or rights.

Libertarianism and the idea of a welfare society are not reconcilable. The market and restricted (limited) constitutional rights cannot guarantee the fulfilment of basic individual and social goals that we all value. The libertarians' futuristic dream of the millenial market-society is not Sen's.

Libertarians have always been meticulous in delimiting human rights to be concerned foremost with the own property-right and the freedom to mind your own business. According to libertarians, rights and freedom are mostly a question of "not having to do with the authorities" and to live free of "governmental interference". But is this really freedom? Is it really a restriction of the freedom of the homeless when the municipality offers him a decent dwelling?

State-intervention does not necessarily mean that our freedoms are restricted. They can, on the contrary, enable and increase real freedom. Talking about freedom *in abstractu* counts for nothing. What really means anything is – as Sen has often stressed – capabilities. What joy does the freedom of movement give the disabled person if no one enables him to use this freedom? What good does it bring us to have freedom of the press if there are no newspapers or journals where we can put forward our views. When estimating welfare more weight should be laid on positive freedom (ability to achieve desired goals) instead of only negative freedom (absence of outer restrictions). Welfare is, as already pointed out in Sen's Tanner Lecture 1979 (Sen [1980]), best understood in terms of capabilities. Positive freedom is a kind of capability to function that has a direct value of its own, while the resources that can increase this capability only get an instrumental value in so far as they help us to achieve that which we really value – our capability to function under different circumstances. It is not possession of commodities or perceived satisfaction that at first hand give a measure of well-being, but our capability to make use of our possessions. To focus on capability means emphasising what goods enable a person to do, and not the goods in themselves. A metric of goods or utilities does not get hold of the fact that the point of our belongings is to create possibilities of choice. Functioning and capability are what matters. What makes us value our car is not the fact that we perhaps own it, but that we can use it to take us where we want to get. Even if freedom is something important in itself, it is most often not for its own sake that we search for it.

Libertarians are oblivious of the fact that some persons' entitlements can restrict the freedom of others, and that the want of property not only restricts the self-determination of the property-less but also makes him an instrument of others' freedom. To this they respond that the more resources there are in society, the more the rich invest their capital to make production effective, and the richer all members of society become. In the libertarian society the egoism of the rich is linked fruitfully with the rest of society.

As Sen has pointed out repeatedly the issue is not only about the size of the cake, but also how to divide it. One cannot get away from the fact that the latter aspect strongly influences people's views on the justification of property-rights.

Unfortunately, the libertarians are often inconsequential when trying to defend their dogma. At first freedom and rights are said to be conceived as having a value of their own – they are holy, inviolable trumps. When shown that this leads to untenable consequences for equality and self-determination of the property-less, they retreat to an economistic viewpoint. Then private ownership, markets and competition are instead defended with utilitarian arguments about rights giving, on the whole, good consequences, that growth increases or some similar argument. The power of the market is made holy in the name of economic efficiency.

But you cannot fall between two stools. Either you stick to liberty and property-rights – like Rand, Locke or Nozick – or you defend laissez-faire capitalism with arguments of economic efficiency – as Hayek and Friedman. Both lines of argumentation are, as shown by Sen, equally weak, but at least have the advantage of being consistent and clear.

To defend property-rights with a reference to an overarching principle of freedom is untenable. *A fortiori* you cannot defend the free market-society with any such principle. If free markets are to be judged to give greater freedom or not, depends on what kinds of freedom we are talking about and how they are defined. Private property-rights limit some people's freedom and the welfare state can, in a likewise manner, both ensure and limit the freedom of people. It is cynical to deny that unequal circumstances create injustice. The attempt of neo-liberalism to show that lack of resources and poverty are not a restriction of freedom only shows how weak their defense of the free market is.

The rights-based neo-liberalism – libertarianism – is basically a political-economic philosophy that defends the freedom of markets and perceives all social welfare policies and tax-based social redistribution attempts as a violation of inalienable human rights. These rights are so strong and far-reaching that state-intervention is equalled to forced labour and theft. If each and every one has the right to his property, the distributions that come about via the free exchanges of the market are just and in no need of re-distributive policies. The state shall only be a minimal state – subordinated to the market – and without other ambitions than upholding law and order.

That the libertarians' catalogue of rights is limited to encompass only liberty and property-rights is no accident. If it were enlarged to also comprise e. g. welfare, the theory would be self-contradictory since property-rights could no more be said to be self-evidently superior to welfare. To neo-liberals every redistribution of welfare that sets aside property-rights is indefensible. But, as Sen over and over has asked, why should property-rights be put above our rights to medical attention, education and health? To most of us it is self-evident that safeguarding possibilities to a decent life can demand redistribution and that a meaningful freedom presupposes that we can develop our capabilities and partake of the welfare of society. Freedom has to be about something more than property. It is not only about want of coercion, but about creating equal opportunities for everyone to lead a good life.

The economistic tradition

Within the economistic tradition, private property, markets and free competition are not defended with arguments based upon the theory of original appropriation, but with utilitarian arguments. The different manifestations of the tradition up until present day neo-Austrians and monetarists all take as their starting points Adam Smith's discussion of the "invisible hand" and "natural freedom".

Adam Smith and the invisible hand

Adam Smith was, like the other Scottish enlightenment philosophers, strongly influenced by the natural rights philosophy. Locke, under the influence of Hugo Grotius and Samuel von Pufendorf, had emphasised people's natural freedom and right against the state. To Smith natural freedom meant, among other things, that the individual himself should have the right to decide for himself where to live and what occupation to take up. The legal system of society should protect people's natural rights.

Smith combined Locke's political liberalism with his own economic liberalism. To many he therefore became the great prophet of capitalism and free markets.

But, as Sen has repeatedly pointed out, Smith was no dogmatic free-market advocate who saw the unrestricted market as a sacred cow. Liberty was the basic principle, but, where needed for the sake of the best of the individual or society, he could think of accepting limitations of freedom. Smith was a liberal in the meaning that if the state interfered, it had to be well motivated.

Normally there was no conflict between the individual's own interests and the common good of the state [Smith (1776:26-27)]: "It is not from the benevolence of the butcher, the brewer, or the baker, that we expect our dinner, but from their regard to their own interest." When the individual only looks to his own interests it is as if he is [Smith (1776:456)] "led by an invisible hand to promote an end which was no part of his intention".

The principle of the invisible hand, however, did not make Smith shut his eyes to the need for a more visible hand to act when so needed. When natural freedom jeopardised the existence and welfare of society, it had to be limited. The invisible hand is not perfect. It sometimes trembles and then society (the state) has to intervene.

In *On Ethics and Economics* Sen [1987:28] writes: "The support that believers in, and advocates of, self-interested behaviour have sought in Adam Smith is, in fact, hard to find on a wider and less biased reading of Smith. The professor of moral philosophy and the pioneer economist did not, in fact, lead a life of spectacular schizophrenia. Indeed, it is precisely the narrowing of the broad Smithian view of human beings, in modern economics, that can be seen as one of the major deficiencies of contemporary economic theory."

On the use and misuse of theories and models in economics

According to Sen, it is important to dispute the common description of Adam Smith as a single-minded prophet of self-interest. Although Smith was right to point out that beneficial exchanges on the market did not need any other motivational force than "self-love", he did emphasise other and broader motivations when dealing with problems of distribution and justice. Sen [200:272] writes: "In these broader contexts, while prudence remained 'of all virtues that which is most helpful to the individual', he explained why 'humanity, generosity, and public spirit', are the qualities most useful to others."

And just like Smith, Sen argues against those neo-liberals that maintain that the market has a value of its own, independently of its effects on people's welfare. As he has shown repeatedly in his studies of famines, the moral status of the market mechanism has to be related to the consequences of the market. If these are good or bad is a question of empirical judgement, not of *a priori* foundational judgement.

Neo-Austrian economics and public-choice theory

One of the most important problems within the social sciences is how to explain how order can emerge from all the different individuals' plans and actions. How shall all the knowledge that is scattered around among the individuals come to the favour of all of us? According to the neo-Austrian philosopher and economist Friedrich von Hayek − under the influence of David Hume and Adam Smith's "invisible hand" − this mainly comes about as the result of a spontaneous order emanating from nature. Contrary to organisations, it does not have any goals and is not intentionally rational. Its main merit is its capacity to economise on the dispersed information.

Hayek uses this theory to explain the evolution of society's institutions, especially its legal rules, which he maintains have largely emerged spontaneously. The systems of rule that shows themselves not to be effective are selected away during the process of evolution and replaced by more effective ones. This thought that evolution should point towards higher and higher efficiency is also an integral part of Hayek's defence of capitalism and a free market society.

Neoliberalism and neoclassical economics

Politically the neo-Austrians represent an extreme form of individualism that is common in neo-liberalism. Like the harmony economists of the 19th century it is maintained that free choices on the market create the best of all worlds. If you just let the free market carry on its own business without an intervening state, a social optimum is spontaneously created. As Sen has hinted at on many occasions, this market ideology can be questioned for expressing wishful political thinking rather than scientific and historical analysis. And commenting on Hayek's championing of "unintended consequences," Sen [2000:257] has to confess that the recognition that many consequences are entirely unintended "can scarcely be seen as a momentous thought".

Another exponent of neo-liberalism, the public choice theory, maintains that political decision-processes can be analysed in the same way as economic theory analyses individual consumers and firms. Just as these are governed by egotistical interests, politicians and other public decision-makers are governed by their endeavour to further their own interests. The will to be re-elected and exercise power makes these groups try to use and manipulate the political system for their own benefit.

According to the public choice theory, man is a rational, egotistic utility-maximiser. This applies both within economy and politics. Both in the election bureau and in the supermarket, man is as consumer and voter basically the same. Critics of the theory, like Sen, have argued that individuals, contrary to this assumption, can, and often do, behave altruistically when making both market and political choices.

Public choice-theorists hold the view that total unanimity reigns on the market, since a free contract between two parts implies that both are satisfied with the conditions. The market, a fortiori, fulfils the demands of democracy better than majority-decisions do.

Unanimous decisions should always be carried out – public choice theorists maintain – since they are economically effective in the sense that someone is better off without anyone else being worse off. At the same time unanimity is considered a guarantee for an individualistic liberty-principle of a liberal type, since no majority can force a minority to change in a personal matter.

As Sen, however, has been able to show, it is not always possible to construct a social welfare function that fulfils both these conditions (of Pareto optimality and liberty). Public choice theorists have tried to find a way out of this conflict by permitting people, through a kind of contractual procedure, to abstain from their freedom of choice for a compensation. This contractual theory can, however, be questioned on the same grounds, since the contract implies that the individuals' freedom of choice is restricted. An individual may certainly *prefer* a special contract-construction, but since it means a selling out of his own freedom he may still not want to *make choices* based on such a preference.

Freedoms and capabilities

Sen has suggested that in judgements of welfare greater attention should be paid to positive freedom (capacity to reach sought-for goals) than negative freedom (non-existence of external restrictions).

The negative concept of liberty has especially been propounded by neo-liberals, while the positive concept has a stronger position in liberal and socialist traditions. What Sen is doing, is to rejuvenate the discussion by implanting a new precision of the concept of positive liberty by his concept of capability. Economists usually measure welfare in terms of what people do or have, but Sen [2000:292] convincingly shows that welfare-measurement also has to include considerations of what people *can* do: "Indeed, sometimes a person may have a very strong reason to have an option precisely for the purpose of rejecting it. For example, when Mahatma Gandhi fasted to make a political point against the Raj, he was not merely starving, he was rejecting the option of eating." People value freedoms, and, as in his contributions to social choice theory, Sen has here explicitly introduced the value of freedom into the issue. To Sen [2000:14], just as to Aristotle, "the usefulness of wealth lies in the things that it allows us to do – the substantive freedoms it helps us to achieve."

This may seem to be a neo-liberal argument, but as we have seen it is not, since Sen's concept of freedoms is quite different to the neo-liberal. Superficially Sen's avowal of freedom(s) as a foundational ethical premise may be reminiscent of libertarianism's strong dedication to unrestricted "freedom", but they are in fact completely different animals. To Sen freedom involves both a *process aspect* and an *opportunity aspect*, while libertarians most often confine freedom to the first aspect and do not care if disadvantaged people suffer from systematic deprivation of substantive opportunities or nor. To Sen [2000:8] economic unfreedom, e.g., "can make a person a helpless prey in the violation of other kinds of freedom." The opportunity and the process aspects do not always go together, and then much of our valuation depends on which aspect we consider most important.

When it comes to what variables should be included in the grounds for judging, he means that goods only have an instrumental value and not an inherent one. The judgement of welfare therefore has to transcend traditional measures, which only consider possession of goods and real incomes. Sen already suggested in *Commodities and Capabilities* (1985) that welfare should be measured in terms of the concept of capability. To Sen, positive freedom is a kind of capability to function that has a direct value of its own, while those resources that can increase this capability only become instrumental in so far as they help to achieve what we really value – namely our capability to function. Contrary to Rawls, Sen holds the view that the possession of primary goods (rights, income, right of self-determination, etc.) is not a good indicator of well-being and freedom. Sick and disabled people may, for example, have bigger problems in functioning than healthy/able-bodied people. Systematic differences that have to do with age and propensity to get sick, imply that possession of primary goods becomes an inaccurate indicator of well-being. Measures of living-standards and welfare-indexes should foremost take into account people's possibilities of acting and developing their capabilities.

In Sen's approach freedom has a value of its own that it often does not have in standard economic theory. According to the latter, e.g., the withdrawal of non-optimal alternatives does not mean a loss, while Sen emphasises that the freedom to be able to choose has a value in itself, and that restricting the set of choices therefore is negative, and should not be neglected in the analysis. Freedom also encompasses the possibility that stands open to the individual, and not that which the individual happens to choose. Capabilities contribute directly to making a person's life richer by extending the opportunities of choice or giving him more "effective freedom".

A pervading trait of Sen's thoughts is that he maintains that traditional welfare theory has gone too far in its frugality in the realm of the information you can include into the theory. The self-imposed lack of information is the main reason for the theory's incapacity to tackle the big and important problems regarding welfare-judgements on both an individual and social level.

Sen shows that the informational base for the libertarian class of rules for deciding on ethical matters is extremely limited. It is obviously inadequate for making informed judgements about problems of well-being and justice. We cannot really make value-judgements with so little information.

Much of Sen's later work has been centred on exactly how one can consistently and with distinction provide the theory with more information and make it more relevant for solving real-world problems. In regard to libertarianism Sen [2000:66-67] writes:

> The uncompromising priority of libertarian rights can be particularly problematic since the actual consequences of the operation of these entitlements can, quite possibly, include rather terrible results. It can, in particular, lead to the violation of the substantive freedom of individuals to achieve those things to which they have reason to attach great importance... The destitutes such as the unemployed or the impoverished may starve precisely because their 'entitlements' – legitimate as they are – do not give them enough food... In terms of its informational basis, libertarianism as an approach is just too limited. Not only does it ignore those variables to which utilitarian and welfarist theories attach great importance, but it also neglects the most basic freedoms that we have reason to treasure and demand.

There is no royal road to evaluations of justice and welfare, and much of the debate on existing alternatives of evaluation is really about what priorities should be made and on what should be at the core of such normative issues. Sen has shown that the priorities that are made could be brought out and analysed through analysing the information that the different approaches and their evaluative judgements are based on. His own capability approach resists the libertarian temptation to treat the freedom-based perspective as an all-or-non form. In fact, he says [Sen 2000:86), in many "practical problems, the possibility of using an explicit freedom-based approach may be relatively limited." Therefore a useful and constructive theory of justice and welfare has to consider both foundational and pragmatic issues. Libertarianism does not and has consequently a short reach. Sen's capability approach does and has consequently an extensive reach. Instead of libertarianism's utopia (dystopia) of some absolute and abstract "freedom", Sen offers a practically fruitful criterion for a theory of justice and welfare.

Human rights

Neo-liberals are often sceptical about talk of human rights since it is not possible, so it is said, to specify whose duty it is to guarantee the fulfilment of these rights. It is held to be impossible to be sure that these rights are realised since they are not matched by corresponding duties.

Sen [2000:230] is sceptical about this argumentation. In normative discussions "rights are often championed as entitlements or powers or immunities that it would be good for people to have. Human rights are seen as rights shared by all – irrespective of citizenship – the benefits of which everyone *should* have." The claims of human rights are addressed generally, and no particular person may be charged to bring about the fulfilment of them. Even though some rights may end up being unfulfilled, it is surely possible for us to distinguish between a right that a person has which has not been fulfilled and a right that the person does not have.

Conclusion

Libertarians often contrast the importance of equality with that of liberty. But to Sen [1992:22-23] it can never be a question of liberty *or* equality. To pose the question in terms of this contrast is according to him a "category mistake". Liberty is among "the possible fields of application of equality, and equality is among the possible patterns of distribution of liberty."

There is a large diversity of spaces in which equality may be demanded. Therefore one has to ask "equality of what?" and then focus on some space that one considers particularly important. Only after fixing the "focal variable", can we get a specific definition of equality. Of course this plurality of spaces is not unique to equality, applying as it does to concepts such as freedom, rights, efficiency and so forth.

To show that freedom of choice means something Sen [1992:38] distinguishes between the "selection view" and the "options view". In contrast to traditional welfare economics, Sen suggests that if we are interested in the freedom of choice "we have to look at the *choices* that the person does in fact have" and not just focus on the particular choice made.

Sen, with his capability approach, explicitly acknowledges human diversity in a way that is impossible within the libertarian approach. Although he is fully aware of the incentive problem – and that therefore the demands of equality have to be supplemented by efficiency considerations – he [Sen (1992:22-23)] argues that the recognition of deep human diversity "may have the effect of restraining the force of the incentive problem".

Sen's concept of capabilities is close to Berlin's defence of positive freedom and has strong implications for our view of people's autonomy. We value rights like freedom in Berlin's positive sense since they reflect our interest in autonomy. To neo-liberals it is freedom in the negative sense that is basic. To Sen, there is a fundamental difference between *formal* and *substantive* freedoms that hinges on the issue of how one converts resources into freedom. This is an issue to which neo-liberals have not paid any attention, and for which Sen also rightly criticises them.

The limits of marginal productivity theory

Thomas Piketty's book *Capital in the twenty-first century* is in many ways an impressive *magnum opus*. It's a wide-ranging and weighty book, almost 700 pages thick, containing an enormous amount of empirical material on the distribution of income and wealth for almost all developed countries in the world for the last one and a half centuries.

But it does not stop at this massive amount of data. Piketty also theorizes and tries to interpret the trends in the presented historical time series data. One of the more striking – and debated – trends that emerges from the data is a kind of generalized U-shaped Kuznets curve for the shares of the top 10 % and top 1 % of wealth and income, showing extremely high values for the period up to the first world war, and then dropping until the 1970/80s, when they – especially in the top 1% – start to rise sharply.

Contrary to Kuznets's (1955) original hypothesis, there does not seem to be any evidence for the idea that income differences should diminish *pari passu* with economic development. The gains that the increase in productivity has led to, has far from been distributed evenly in society. The optimistic view on there being automatic income and wealth equalizers, commonly held among growth and development economists until a few years ago, has been proven unwarranted.

So, then, why have income differences more or less exploded since the 1980s?

On the illusions of "marginal productivity"

In my own country, Sweden, it is pretty obvious that we need to weigh in institutional, political and social forces to explain the extraordinary increase in the functional income inequality distribution. Not the least changes in the wage negotiation system, weakened trade unions, the new "independent" role of the central bank (Riksbanken) and it's single-mindedly rigid focus on price stability, a new tax-system, globalization, financialization of the economy, neoliberal "Thatcher-Reagan" deregulations of markets, etc., etc., have profoundly influenced wealth and income distribution. What was once an egalitarian Swedish model, has during the last three decades been reduced to something more akin to the rest of continental Europe, with sharply increased income differences (especially incomes from owning capital and trading financial assets). It is difficult to imagine a sustainable explanation for the falling wages share since the 1980s – not only in Sweden, but in virtually all developed countries – that does not to a large part take account of the fight over distribution between classes in an ongoing restructuring of our society and its underlying fundamental socio-economic relationships.

Mainstream economics textbooks – Mankiw & Taylor (2011) is a typical example – usually refer to the interrelationship between technological development and education as the main causal force behind the increased inequality. If the educational system (supply) develops at the same pace as the technology (demand), there should be no increase, *ceteris paribus*, in the ratio between high-income (highly educated) groups and low-income (low education) groups. In the race between technology and education, the proliferation of skilled-biased technological change has, however, allegedly increased the premium for the highly educated group.

Another prominent explanation is that globalization – in accordance with Ricardo's theory of comparative advantage and the Wicksell-Heckscher-Ohlin-Stolper-Samuelson factor price theory – has benefited capital in the advanced countries and labour in the developing countries. The problem with these theories are *inter alia* that they *explicitly* assume full employment and international immobility of the factors of production. Globalization means more than anything else that capital and labour have to a large extent become mobile over country borders. These mainstream trade theories are *a fortiori* really not applicable in the world of today, and they are certainly not able to explain the international trade pattern that has developed during the last decades. Although it seems as though capital in the developed countries has benefited from globalization, it is difficult to detect a similar positive effect on workers in the developing countries (Altvater & Mahnkopf 2002).

The limits of marginal productivity theory

As Piketty shows, there are, however, also some other quite obvious problems with these kinds of inequality explanations. The impressively vast databank of information on income and inequality that Piketty has created – especially *The World Top Incomes Database* – shows, as noted, that the increase in incomes has been concentrated especially in the top 1%. If education was the main reason behind the increasing income gap, one would expect a much broader group of people in the upper echelons of the distribution taking part of this increase. It is, as recent research has shown (den Haan 2011), dubious, to say the least, trying to explain, for example, the high wages in the finance sector with a marginal productivity argument. High-end wages seem to be more a result of pure luck or membership of the same "club" as those who decide on the wages and bonuses, than of "marginal productivity."

Mainstream economics, with its technologically determined marginal productivity theory, seems to be difficult to reconcile with reality. But walked-out Harvard economist and George Bush advisor, Greg Mankiw (2011), does not want to give up on his preferred theory that easily:

> Even if the income gains are in the top 1 percent, why does that imply that the right story is not about education?

> If indeed a year of schooling guaranteed you precisely a 10 percent increase in earnings, then there is no way increasing education by a few years could move you from the middle class to the top 1 percent.

> But it may be better to think of the return to education as stochastic. Education not only increases the average income a person will earn, but it also changes the entire distribution of possible life outcomes. It does not guarantee that a person will end up in the top 1 percent, but it increases the likelihood. I have not seen any data on this, but I am willing to bet that the top 1 percent are more educated than the average American; while their education did not ensure their economic success, it played a role.

On the use and misuse of theories and models in economics

A couple of years later Mankiw (2014) makes a new effort at explaining and defending income inequalities, this time invoking Adam Smith's invisible hand:

> [B]y delivering extraordinary performances in hit films, top stars may do more than entertain millions of moviegoers and make themselves rich in the process. They may also contribute many millions in federal taxes, and other millions in state taxes. And those millions help fund schools, police departments and national defense for the rest of us...

> [T]he richest 1 percent aren't motivated by an altruistic desire to advance the public good. But, in most cases, that is precisely their effect.

Mankiw's card-carrying neoclassical apologetics reminds of John Bates Clark's (1899) argument that marginal productivity results in an ethically just distribution. But that is not something – even if it were true – we could confirm empirically, since it is impossible *realiter* to separate out what is the marginal contribution of any factor of production. The hypothetical *ceteris paribus* addition of only one factor in a production process is often heard of in textbooks, but never seen in reality.

When reading Mankiw on the "just desert" of the 0.1 %, one gets a strong feeling that he is ultimately trying to argue that a market economy is some kind of moral free zone where, if left undisturbed, people get what they "deserve". To most social scientists that probably smacks more of being an evasive action trying to explain away a very disturbing structural "regime shift" that has taken place in our societies. A shift that has very little to do with "stochastic returns to education". Those were in place also 30 or 40 years ago. At that time they meant that perhaps a top corporate manager earned 10-20 times more what "ordinary" people earned. Today it means that they earn 100-200 times more what "ordinary" people earn. A question of education? Hardly. It is probably more a question of greed and a lost sense of a common project of building a sustainable society. Or as the always eminently quotable Robert Solow (2014a) puts it:

The limits of marginal productivity theory

Who could be against allowing people their 'just deserts?' But there is that matter of what is 'just'. Most serious ethical thinkers distinguish between deservingness and happenstance. Deservingness has to be rigorously earned. You do not 'deserve' that part of your income that comes from your parents' wealth or connections or, for that matter, their DNA. You may be born just plain gorgeous or smart or tall, and those characteristics add to the market value of your marginal product, but not to your deserts. It may be impractical to separate effort from happenstance numerically, but that is no reason to confound them, especially when you are thinking about taxation and redistribution. That is why we want to temper the wind to the shorn lamb, and let it blow on the sable coat.

Since the race between technology and education does not seem to explain the new growing income gap – and even if technological change has become more and more capital augmenting, it is also quite clear that not only the wages of low-skilled workers have fallen, but also the overall wage share – mainstream economists increasingly refer to "meritocratic extremism," "winners-take-all markets" (Frank & Cook 1995) and "super star-theories" (Rosen 1981) for explanation. But this is also – as noted by Piketty (2014:334) – highly questionable:

> The most convincing proof of the failure of corporate governance and of the absence of a rational productivity justification for extremely high executive pay is that when we collect data about individual firms... it is very difficult to explain the observed variations in terms of firm performance. If we look at various performance indicators, such as sales growth, profits, and so on, we can break down the observed variance as a sum of other variances: variance due to causes external to the firm... plus other "nonexternal" variances. Only the latter can be significantly affected by the decisions of the firm's managers. If executive pay were determined by marginal productivity, one would expect its variance to have little to do with external variances and to

depend solely or primarily on nonexternal variances. In fact,
we observe just the opposite.

Fans may want to pay extra to watch top-ranked athletes or movie stars
performing on television and film, but corporate managers are hardly the
stuff that people's dreams are made of – and they seldom appear on
television and in the movie theaters.

Everyone may prefer to employ the best corporate manager there is, but a
corporate manager, unlike a movie star, can only provide his services to a
limited number of customers. From the perspective of "super-star theories",
a good corporate manager should only earn marginally better than an
average corporate manager. The average earnings of corporate managers
of the 50 biggest Swedish companies today, is equivalent to the wages of 46
blue-collar workers (Bergström & Järliden 2013:10). Executive pay packages
at that outlandish level is, as noted by Solow (2014b:9)

> ... usually determined in a cozy way by boards of directors
> and compensation committees made up of people very like
> the executives they are paying.

It is indeed difficult to see the takeoff of the top executives as anything else
but a reward for being a member of the same illustrious club. That they
should be equivalent to indispensable and fair productive contributions –
marginal products – is straining credulity too far. That so many corporate
managers and top executives make fantastic earnings today, is strong
evidence the theory is patently wrong and basically functions as a
legitimizing device of indefensible and growing inequalities.

Having read Piketty (2014:332) no one ought to doubt that the idea that
capitalism is an expression of impartial market forces of supply and demand,
bears but little resemblance to actual reality:

> It is only reasonable to assume that people in a position to
> set their own salaries have a natural incentive to treat
> themselves generously, or at the very least to be rather
> optimistic in gauging their marginal productivity.

The limits of marginal productivity theory

But although I agree with Piketty on the obvious – at least to anyone not equipped with ideological blinders – insufficiency and limitation of neoclassical marginal productivity theory to explain the growth of top 1 % incomes, I strongly disagree with his rather unwarranted belief that when it comes to more ordinary wealth and income, the marginal productivity theory somehow should still be considered applicable. It is not.

Wealth and income distribution, both individual and functional, in a market society is to an overwhelmingly high degree influenced by institutionalized political and economic norms and power relations, things that have pretty little to do with marginal productivity in complete and profit-maximizing competitive market models – not to mention how extremely difficult, if not outright impossible it is to *empirically* disentangle and measure different individuals' contributions in the typical team work production that characterize modern societies; or, especially when it comes to "capital", what it is supposed to mean and how to measure it. Remunerations, *a fortiori*, do not necessarily correspond to any marginal product of different factors of production – or to "compensating differentials" due to non-monetary characteristics of different jobs, natural ability, effort or chance). As Amartya Sen (1982) writes:

> The personal production view is difficult to sustain in cases of interdependent production... i.e., in almost all the usual cases... A common method of attribution is according to "marginal product"... This method of accounting is internally consistent only under some special assumptions, and the actual earning rates of resource owners will equal the corresponding "marginal products" only under some further special assumptions. But even when all these assumptions have been made... marginal product accounting, when consistent, is useful for deciding how to use additional resources... but it does not "show" which resource has "produced" how much... The alleged fact is, thus, a fiction, and while it might appear to be a convenient fiction, it is more convenient for some than for others...

159

On the use and misuse of theories and models in economics

> The personal production view... confounds the marginal impact with total contribution, glosses over the issues of relative prices, and equates "being more productive" with "owning more productive resources"... An Indian barber or circus performer may not be producing any less than a British barber or circus performer — just the opposite if I am any judge — but will certainly earn a great deal less...

Put simply – highly paid workers and corporate managers are not always highly productive workers and corporate managers, and less highly paid workers and corporate managers are not always less productive. History has over and over again disconfirmed the close connection between productivity and remuneration postulated in mainstream income distribution theory.

Neoclassical marginal productivity theory is a collapsed theory from a both historical and – as shown already by Sraffa in the 1920s, and in the Cambridge capital controversy in the 1960s and 1970s – theoretical point of view. But, unfortunately, Piketty trivializes the concept of capital and the Cambridge controversy over it. As every mainstream textbook on growth theory and most neoclassical economists, Piketty just chooses to turn a blind eye to it and pretend it is much fuss about nothing. But they are wrong.

As Joan Robinson (1953:81) writes:

> The production function has been a powerful instrument of miseducation. The student of economic theory is taught to write $Q = f(L, K)$ where L is a quantity of labor, K a quantity of capital and Q a rate of output of commodities. He is instructed to assume all workers alike, and to measure L in man-hours of labor; he is told something about the index-number problem in choosing a unit of output; and then he is hurried on to the next question, in the hope that he will forget to ask in what units K is measured. Before he ever does ask, he has become a professor, and so sloppy habits of thought are handed on from one generation to the next.

The limits of marginal productivity theory

And as Edwin Burmeister (2000:312) admitted already fifteen years ago:

> It is important, for the record, to recognize that key participants in the debate openly admitted their mistakes. Samuelson's seventh edition of Economics was purged of errors. Levhari and Samuelson published a paper which began, 'We wish to make it clear for the record that the nonreswitching theorem associated with us is definitely false'... Leland Yeager and I jointly published a note acknowledging his earlier error and attempting to resolve the conflict between our theoretical perspectives... However, the damage had been done, and Cambridge, UK, 'declared victory': Levhari was wrong, Samuelson was wrong, Solow was wrong, MIT was wrong and therefore neoclassical economics was wrong. As a result there are some groups of economists who have abandoned neoclassical economics for their own refinements of classical economics. In the United States, on the other hand, mainstream economics goes on as if the controversy had never occurred. Macroeconomics textbooks discuss 'capital' as if it were a well-defined concept – which it is not, except in a very special one-capital-good world (or under other unrealistically restrictive conditions). The problems of heterogeneous capital goods have also been ignored in the 'rational expectations revolution' and in virtually all econometric work.

In a way these deficiencies are typical of Piketty's book – while presenting and analyzing an impressive amount of empirical data, the theory upon which he ultimately grounds his analysis, does not live up to the high standard set by the empirical material.

Piketty (2014:333) is obviously, at least when discussing the remuneration of the top 1 %, aware of some of the limitations of neoclassical marginal productivity theory, but nonetheless, rather unwarranted and without much argumentation, holds it to be applicable to the more ordinary levels of wages and incomes:

To be clear, I am not claiming that all wage inequality is determined by social norms of fair remuneration. As noted, the theory of marginal productivity and of the race between technology and education offers a plausible explanation of the long-run evolution of the wage distribution, at least up to a certain level of pay and within a certain degree of precision. Technology and skills set limits within which most wages must be fixed.

But, of course, once admitting that the top 1% can side-step marginal productivity concerns, the theory is seriously undermined since there is no consistent reason presented to exclude other segments of income earners from having the same degree of freedom. And as already Hicks (1932) pointed out – as long as we only have rather uncertain measures of the elasticity of demand, the marginal productivity theory cannot, anyway, say how the relative shares of incomes will develop.

Conclusion

In an ongoing trend towards increasing inequality in both developing and emerging countries all over the world, wage shares have fallen substantially – and the growth in real wages has lagged far behind the growth in productivity – over the past three decades.

As already Karl Marx argued 150 years ago, the division between profits and wages is ultimately determined by the struggle between classes – something fundamentally different to hypothesized "marginal products" in neoclassical Cobb-Douglas or CES varieties of neoclassical production functions.

Compared to Marx's *Capital*, the one written by Piketty has a much more fragile foundation when it comes to theory. Where Piketty is concentrating on classifying different income and wealth categories, Marx was focusing on the facedown between different classes, struggling to appropriate as large a portion of the societal net product as possible.

The limits of marginal productivity theory

Piketty's painstaking empirical research is, doubtless, very impressive, but his theorizing – although occasionally critical of orthodox economics and giving a rather dismal view of present-day and future capitalism as a rich-get-richer inequality society – is to a large extent shackled by neoclassical economic theory, something that unfortunately makes some of his more central theoretical analyses rather unfruitful from the perspective of realism and relevance.

A society where we allow the inequality of incomes and wealth to increase without bounds, sooner or later implodes. A society that promotes unfettered selfishness as the one and only virtue, erodes the cement that keeps us together, and in the end we are only left with people dipped in the ice cold water of egoism and greed.

If reading Piketty's *magnum opus* get people thinking about these dangerous trends in modern capitalism, it may – in spite of its theoretical limitations – have a huge positive political impact. And that is not so bad. For, as the author of the original *Capital* once famously wrote:

> The philosophers have only interpreted the world, in various
> ways. The point, however, is to change it.

On the use and misuse of theories and models in economics

References

Alexandrova, Anna (2008). Making Models Count. *Philosophy of Science* 75: 383-404

Altvater, Elmar & Mahnkopf, Birgit (2002). *Grenzen der Globalisierung.* Münster: Westfälisches Dampfboot

Arnsperger, Christian & Varoufakis, Yanis (2006). What Is Neoclassical Economics? The three axioms responsible for its theoretical oeuvre, practical irrelevance and, thus, discursive power. *Panoeconomicus* 1:5-18

Arrow, Kenneth (1968). Economic Equilibrium. *International Encyclopedia of the Social Sciences*

Ball, Laurence (1990). Intertemporal Substitution and Constraints on Labor Supply: Evidence From Panel Data. *Economic Inquiry* 28:706-724

Bergström, Jeanette & Järliden Bergström, Åsa-Pia (2013). *Makteliten: klyftorna består.* Stockholm: LO

Bhaskar, Roy (1989).*The possibility of naturalism: a philosophical critique of the contemporary human sciences.* 2. ed. New York: Harvester Wheatsheaf

Bigo, Vinca (2008). Explaining Modern Economics (as a Microcosm of Society). *Cambridge Journal of Economics* 32:527-554

Blaug, Mark (1997). Ugly currents in modern economics. *Policy Options* 17:3-8

Boaz, David (ed.) (1997). *The Libertarian Reader.* The Free Press 1997

Brodbeck, May (1968[1959]). Models, Meaning and Theories, in M. Brodbeck (ed.), *Readings in the Philosophy of the Social Sciences.* New York: Macmillan

Buiter, Willem (2009). The unfortunate uselessness of most 'state of the art' academic monetary economics. *Financial Times.* Blog FT.com/Maverecon.

Burmeister, Edwin (2000). The capital theory controversy, pp. 305-314 in Kurz, Heinz-Dieter (ed.) *Critical essays on Piero Sraffa's legacy in economics.* New York: Cambridge University Press

Cartwright, Nancy (1989). *Nature's Capacities and Their Measurement.* Oxford: Oxford University Press

Cartwright, Nancy (1999). *The Dappled World.* Cambridge: Cambridge University Press

On the use and misuse of theories and models in economics

Cartwright, Nancy (2002). The limits of causal order, from economics to physics. In U. Mäki (ed.), *Fact and fiction in economics* (pp. 137-151). Cambridge: Cambridge University Press

Cartwright, Nancy (2007). *Hunting Causes and UsingThem*. Cambridge: Cambridge University Press.

Cartwright, Nancy (2007). Are RCT's the Gold Standard? *Biosocieties*, 2, 11-20

Cartwright, Nancy (2011). Will this Policy Work for You? Predicting Effectiveness Better: How Philosophy Helps. *Presidential Address, PSA 2010*

Cartwright, Nancy (2009). If no capacities then no credible worlds. But can models reveal capacities? *Erkenntnis* 70:45-58

Cassel, Gustav (1899). Grundriss einer elementaren Preislehre. *Zeitschrift für die gesamte Staatswissenschaft* 55.3:395-458

Chao, Hsiang-Ke (2002). Professor Hendry's Econometric Methodology Reconsidered: Congruence and Structural Empiricism. *CPNSS Technical Report* 20/02

Chatfield, Chris (1995). Model Uncertainty, Data Mining and Statistical Inference. *Journal of the Royal Statistical Society*

Clark, John Bates (1899). *The distribution of wealth: a theory of wages, interest and profits*. New York: Macmillan

Clower, Robert (1989). The State of Economics: Hopeless but not Serious, in *The Spread of Economic Ideas*, (eds.) D. Colander and A. W. Coats, Cambridge University Press

Cournot, Augustin (1838). *Recherches sur les principes mathématiques de la théorie des richesses*. Paris. Translated by N. T. Bacon 1897 as Researches into the Mathematical Principles of the Theory of Wealth. New York: The Macmillan Company

Danermark, Berth et al. (2002). *Explaining society: critical realism in the social sciences*. London: Routledge

Davidson, Paul (1983). Rational expectations: a fallacious foundation for studying crucial decisionmaking processes. *Journal of Post Keynesian Economics* 5

Debreu, Gérard (1974). Excess demand functions. *Journal of Mathematical Economics* 1: 15-21

den Haan, Wouter (2011). Why Do We Need a Financial Sector? *Vox* October 24

References

Estrella, Arturo & Fuhrer, Jeffrey (2002). Dynamic Inconsistencies: Counterfactual Implications of a Class of Rational Expectations Models. *American Economic Review* 92: 1013-28

Evans, George & Honkapohja, Seppo (2001). *Learning and expectations in macroeconomics*. Princeton: Princeton University Press

Fisher, Ronald (1922). On the mathematical foundations of theoretical statistics. *Philosophical Transactions of The Royal Society*

Falk, Armin & Heckman, James (2009). Lab Experiments Are a Major Source of Knowledge in the Social Sciences. *Science* 23 October.

Frank, Robert H. (2010). *Microeconomics and behavior*. 8. ed., International student ed. New York: McGraw-Hill Higher Education

Frank, Robert & Cook, Philip (1995). *The Winner-Take-All Society*. New York: The Free Press.

Freedman, David (2009). *Statistical Models and Causal Inference: A Dialogue with the Social Sciences*. Cambridge: Cambridge University Press.

Freedman, David (2010). *Statistical Models and Causal Inference*. Cambridge: Cambridge University Press

Friedman, Milton (1953). *Essays in Positive Economics*. Chicago: University of Chicago Press

Frydman, Roman & Goldberg, Michael (2007). *Imperfect Knowledge Economics*. Princeton: Princeton University Press

Garfinkel, Alan (1981). *Forms of Explanation*. New Haven: Yale University Press
Gauthier, David (1986). *Morals by Agreement*. Oxford University Press

Gautier, Pieter *et al.* (2012). Estimating equilibrium effects of job search assistance, CEPR Discussion Papers 9066, C.E.P.R. Discussion Papers.

Georgescu-Roegen, Nicholas (1966). Choice, Expectations, and Measurability. In *Analytical Economics: Issues and Problems*. Cambridge, Massachusetts: Harvard University Press

Georgescu-Roegen, Nicholas (1971). *The Entropy Law and the Economic Process*, Harvard University Press

Gibbard, Alan & Varian, Hal (1978). Economic Models. *Journal of Philosophy* 75: 664-77

167

On the use and misuse of theories and models in economics

Gordon Robert J. (2009) Is Modern Macro or 1978-era Macro more Relevant to the understanding of the Current Economic Crisis? http://faculty-web.at.northwestern.edu/economics/gordon/GRU_Combined_090909.pdf

Granger, Clive (2004). Critical realism and econometrics: an econometrician's view. In P. Lewis (ed.), *Transforming Economics: Perspectives on the critical realist project* (pp.96-106). London: Routledge

Grüne-Yanoff, Till (2009). Learning from Minimal Economic Models. *Erkenntnis* 70:81-99 Haavelmo, Trygve (1943). Statistical testing of business-cycle theories. *The Review of Economics and Statistics* 25:13-18

Grüne-Yanoff, Till (1944). The probability approach in econometrics. Supplement to *Econometrica* 12:1-115

Hahn, Frank (1994). An Intellectual Retrospect. *Banca Nazionale del Lavoro Quarterly Review* XLVIII:245–58

Hahn, Frank (2005). An interview with Frank Hahn on the occasion of his 80th birthday. *Storia del pensiero economico* 2

Hájek, Alan (1997). What Conditional Probability Could Not Be. MS, California Institute of Technology.

Hansen, Lars Peter & Heckman, James (1996). The Empirical Foundations of Calibration. *Journal of Economic Perspectives* 10:87-104

Harman, Gilbert (1965). The Inference to the Best Explanation. *The Philosophical Review* 74:88-95

Hartley, James (1997).*The representative agent in macroeconomics*. London: Routledge

Hausman, Daniel (1997). Why Does Evidence Matter So Little To Economic Theory?

In Dalla Chiara et al (eds.), *Structures and Norms in Science* (pp 395-407). Dordrecht: Reidel

In Dalla Chiara et al (2001). Explanation and Diagnosis in Economics. *Revue Internationale De Philosophie* 55:311-326

Hayek, Friedrich von (1974). *The Pretence of Knowledge*. Nobel Memorial Lecture. http://nobelprize.org/nobel_prizes/economics/laureates/1974/hayek-lecture.html

Heckman, James (2005). The Scientific Model of Causality. Sociological Methodology 35

Hendry, David (1983). On Keynesian model building and the rational expectations critique: a question of methodology. *Cambridge Journal of Economics*

References

Hendry, David (1995). *Dynamic Econometrics*. Oxford: Oxford University Press

Hendry, David (1997). The role of econometrics in scientific economics. In A. d'Autome & J A Cartelier (eds), *Is Economics Becoming a Hard Science*. Cheltenham, Edward Elgar

Hendry, David (2000 (1993)), *Econometrics: Alchemy or Science?* 2nd edition. Oxford: Oxford University Press

Hicks, John (1932). *The theory of wages*. London: Macmillan

Hicks, John (1956). *A Revision of Demand Theory*. Oxford: Clarendon Press

Hicks, John (1979). *Causality in Economics*. New York: Basic Books.

Hicks, John (1984). Is Economics a Science? *Interdisciplinary Science Review* 9:213-219

Hoover, Kevin (1988). *The New Classical Macroeconomics*. Oxford: Basil Blackwell

Hoover, Kevin (2001). *The methodology of empirical macroeconomics*. Cambridge: Cambridge University Press

Hoover, Kevin (2002), Econometrics and reality. In U. Mäki (ed.), *Fact and fiction in economics* (pp. 152-177). Cambridge: Cambridge University Press

Hoover, Kevin (2009). Microfoundations and the ontology of macroeconomics. In H. Kincaid and D. Ross (eds), *The Oxford Handbook of Philosophy of Economics*, Oxford: Oxford University Press.

Hoover, Kevin (2010a). Microfoundational Programs (January 14, 2010). http://dx.doi.org/10.2139/ssrn.1562282

Hoover, Kevin (2010b). Idealizing Reduction: The Microfoundations of Macroeconomics. *Erkenntnis* 73

Hoover, Kevin (2013a). Rational Expectations: Retrospect and Prospect: A Panel Discussion with Michael Lovell, Robert Lucas, Dale Mortensen, Robert Shiller, and Neil Wallace. In *Macroeconomic Dynamics* 5:1169-1192

Hoover, Kevin (2013b). Foundations or Bridges? A Review of J.E. King's the Mocrofoundations Delusion: Metaphor and Dogma in the History of Macroeconomics (August 23, 2013). http://dx.doi.org/10.2139/ssrn.2317947

Houthakker, Hendrik (1950). Revealed Preference and the Utility Function. *Economica* 17 (May):159-74

Houthakker, Hendrik (1961). The Present State of Consumption Theory. *Econometrica* 29 (October):704-40

169

Janssen, Maarten (2006), Microfoundations. http://dx.doi.org/10.2139/ssrn.901163

Jespersen, Jesper (2009). *Macroeconomic Methodology*. Cheltenham: Edward Elgar

Jones, Charles (2010). *Macroeconomics: economic crisis update*. New York: W. W. Norton

Kahneman, Daniel (2011). *Thinking, fast and slow*. 1.ed. New York: Farrar, Straus and Giroux

Kelly, John L. (1956). A New Interpretation of Information Rate. *Bell System Technical Journal* 35:917-926

Keuzenkamp, Hugo (2000). *Probability, econometrics and truth*. Cambridge: Cambridge University Press.

Keynes, John Maynard (1936). *The general theory of employment, interest and money*. London: MacMillan

Keynes, John Maynard (1937). The General Theory of Employment. *Quarterly Journal of Economics* 51:209-23

Keynes, John Maynard (1939). Preface to the French edition of General Theory. http://gutenberg.net.au/ebooks03/0300071h/printall.html

Keynes, John Maynard (1939), Professor Tinbergen's method. *Economic Journal* 49:558-68

Keynes, John Maynard (1951 (1926)). *Essays in Biography*. London: Rupert Hart-Davis

Keynes, John Maynard (1964 (1936)). *The General Theory of Employment, Interest, and Money*. London: Harcourt Brace Jovanovich

Keynes, John Maynard (1971-89). *The Collected Writings of John Maynard Keynes*, vol. I-XXX, D E Moggridge & E A G Robinson (eds). London: Macmillan

Keynes, John Maynard (1973 (1921)). *A Treatise on Probability*. Volume VIII of The Collected Writings of John Maynard Keynes, London: Macmillan

King, John Edward (2012). *The microfoundations delusion: metaphor and dogma in the history of macroeconomics*. Cheltenham: Edward Elgar

Kirman, Alan (1989). The intrinsic limits of modern economic theory: the emperor has no clothes. *Economic Journal* 99

Kirman, Alan (1992). Whom or what does the representative individual represent? *Journal of Economic Perspectives* 6:117-136

Knight, Frank (1921). *Risk, Uncertainty and Profit*, Boston: Houghton Mifflin

References

Knuuttila, Tarja (2009). Isolating Representations Versus Credible Constructions? Economic Modelling in Theory and Practice. *Erkenntnis* 70:59-80

Kornai, Janos (1971). *Anti-equilibrium*. London: North-Holland

Kreps, David (1990). *A Course in Microeconomic Theory*. New York: Harvester Wheatsheaf.

Krugman, Paul (2000). How complicated does the model have to be? *Oxford Review of Economic Policy* 16:33-42

Krugman, Paul (2009). How Did Economists Get It So Wrong? *The New York Times* September 6

Kuorikoski, Jaakko & Lehtinen, Aki (2009). Incredible Worlds, Credible Results. *Erkenntnis* 70:119-131

Kuznets, Simon (1955). Economic Growth and Income Inequality. *American Economic Review*, pp. 1-28

Lawson, Tony (1989). Realism and instrumentalism in the development of Econometrics. *Oxford Economic Papers* 41:236-258

Lawson, Tony (1997). *Economics and Reality*. London: Routledge

Lawson, Tony (2003). *Reorienting Economics*. London: Routledge

Leamer, Edward (2010). Tantalus on the Road to Asymptopia, *Journal of Economic Perspectives* 24:31-46

Levine, David K (2012). Why Economists Are Right: Rational Expectations and the Uncertainty Principle in Economics, *Huffington Post* http://www.huffingtonpost.com/david-k-levine/uncertainty-principle

Levitt, Steven & List, John (2009). Field experiments in economics: The past, the present, and the future, *European Economic Review* 53:1-18

Lieberson, Stanley (1985). *Making it count: the improvement of social research and theory*, Berkeley: University of California Press

Lipton, Peter (2004). *Inference to the Best Explanation*. 2nd ed, London: Routledge Louçã, Franciso (2007). *The Years of High Econometrics: A Short History of the Generation that reinvented economics*. Abingdon: Routledge

Lucas, Robert (1972). Expectations and the neutrality of money. *Journal of Economic Theory 4*

Lucas, Robert (1981). *Studies in Business-Cycle Theory*. Oxford: Basil Blackwell

Lucas, Robert (1986). Adaptive Behavior and Economic Theory. In Hogarth, Robin & Reder, Melvin (eds.) *Rational Choice* (pp. 217-242). Chicago: The University of Chicago Press

Lucas, Robert (1987). *Models of Business Cycles*. Oxford: Basil Blackwell.

Lucas, Robert (1988), What Economists Do.
http://home.uchicago.edu/~vlima/courses/econ203/fall01/Lucas_wedo.pdf

Lucas, Robert (1995). The Monetary Neutrality. The Nobel Lecture, Stockholm: The Nobel Foundation

Mankiw, Gregory (2011). Educating Oligarchs. *Greg Mankiw's blog*, November 5

Mankiw, Gregory (2014). Yes, the Wealthy Can Be Deserving, *New York Times*, February 15

Mankiw, Gregory & Taylor, Mark (2011). *Economics*. Andover: South-Western Cengage Learning

Mantel, Rolf (1974). On the characterization of aggregate excess demand. *Journal of Economic Theory* 7: 348–353

Marshall, Alfred (1951(1885)). *The Present Position of Economics*, Inaugural Lecture at Cambridge, cited in Keynes, *Essays in Biography*, London:Rupert Hart-Davis

Mas-Collel, Andreu et al. (1995). *Microeconomic Theory*. New York: Oxford University Press

Meeusen, Wim (2011). Whither the Microeonomic Foundations of Macroeconomic Theory? *Brussels Economic Review* 54

Mencken, Henry Louis (1917). The Divine Afflatus. *New York Evening Mail*. November 16

Moses, Jonathan & Knutsen, Torbjörn (2007). *Ways of Knowing*. New York: Palgrave

Muth, John (1961). Rational expectations and the theory of price movements. *Econometrica* 29

Mäki, Uskali (2009), MISSing the World. Models as Isolations and Credible Surrogate Systems. *Erkenntnis* 70:29-43

Mäki, Uskali (2011). Models and the locus of their truth. *Synthese* 180:47-63

Nelson, Alan (1984). Some issues surrounding the reduction of macroeconomics to microeconomics. *Philosophy of Science* 51

Nozick, Robert (1974). *Anarchy, State, and Utopia*. Oxford: Blackwell

References

Piketty, Thomas (2014). *Capital in the twenty-first century.* Cambridge, Mass.: Belknap Press

Pratten, Stephen (2005). Economics as progress: the LSE approach to econometric modeling and critical realism as programmes for research. *Cambridge Journal of Economics* 29:179-205

Prescott, Edward (1977). Should Control Theory be Used for Economic Stabilization? In K. Brunner and A. H. Meltzer (eds) *Optimal Policies, Control Theory and Technology Exports*, Carnegie- Rochester Conference Series on Public Policy, volume 7, Amsterdam:

Qin, Duo (2013). *A History of Econometrics: The Reformation from the 1970s.* Oxford: Oxford University Press.

Robinson, Joan (1953). The Production Function and the Theory of Capital. *Review of Economic Studies*, pp. 81-106

Rosenberg, Alexander (1978). The Puzzle of Economic Modeling. *Journal of Philosophy* 75:679-83.

Rosen, Sherwin (1981). The Economics of Superstars. *American Economic Review* pp. 845-858

Salmon, Wesley (1971). Statistical Explanation. In W. Salmon (ed.), *Statistical Explanation and Statistical Relevance.* Pittsburgh: University of Pittsburgh Press

Salsburg, David (2001). *The Lady Tasting Tea.* Henry Holt

Samuelson, Paul (1938). A Note on the Pure Theory of Consumer's Behaviour. *Economica* 5:61-71

Samuelson, Paul (1938a). A Note on the Pure Theory of Consumer's Behaviour: An Addendum. *Economica* 5:353-4

Samuelson, Paul (1947). *Foundations of Economic Analysis.* Cambridge, Massachusetts: Harvard University Press

Samuelson, Paul (1948). Consumption Theory in Terms of Revealed Preference. *Economica* 15:243-53

Samuelson, Paul (1950). The Problem of Integrability in Utility Theory. *Economica* 17:355-85

Samuelson, Paul (1953). Consumption Theorems in Terms of Overcompensation rather than Indifference Comparisons. *Economica* 20:1-9

Samuelson, Paul (1964). Theory and Realism: A Reply. *American Economic Review* 54:736-39

On the use and misuse of theories and models in economics

Savage, L. J. (1954). *The Foundations of Statistics.* John Wiley and Sons, New York

Sayer, Andrew (2000). *Realism and Social Science.* London: SAGE Publications

Searle, John (1996[1995]). *The construction of social reality.* London: Penguin
Seidman, Laurence (2005), The New Classical Counter-Revolution: A False Path for
Macro-economics. *Eastern Economic Journal* 31:131-40

Sen, Amartya (1980). Equality of What? In Sterling McMurrin (ed,), The Tanner
Lectures on Human Values vol. I Salt Lake City 1980

Sen, Amartya (1982a). *Choice, Welfare and Measurement.* London: Basil Blackwell

Sen, Amartya (1982b). Just deserts. *New York Review of Books*, March 4

Sen, Amartya (1985). *Commodities and Capabilities.* Amsterdam: North-Holland

Sen, Amartya (1992). *Inequality Reexamined.* Cambridge: Harvard University Press

Sen, Amartya (1987). *On Ethics & Economics.* Oxford: Blackwell

Sen, Amartya (2000). *Development as Freedom.* New York: Anchor Books

Sen, Amartya (2008). The Discipline of Economics. *Economica* 75:617-628

Shackle, G. L. S. (1972). *Epistemics & Economics: A Critique of Economic Doctrines.*
Cambridge: Cambridge University Press

Siakantaris, Nikos (2000). Experimental economics under the microscope.
Cambridge Journal of Economics 24:267-281

Simon, Herbert (1963). Problems of methodology. *American Economic Review*
53:229-31

Singer, Maxine (1997). Thoughts of a nonmillenarian. *Bulletin of the American
Academy of Arts and Sciences* 51:36-51

Sippel, Reinhard 1997. An experiment on the pure theory of consumer's behaviour.
Economic Journal 107:1431-44.

Smith, Vernon (1982). Microeconomic systems as experimental science. *American
Economic Review* 72:923-55.

Snowdon, Brian & Vane, Howard (1998). Transforming macroeconomics: an
interview with Robert E Lucas Jr. *Journal of Economic Methodology* 5

Solow, Robert (2010). Testimony to Congress given to the House Committee on
Science and Technology.
http://science.house.gov/publications/hearings_markups_details.aspx?NewsID=2876

References

Solow, Robert (2014a). Correspondence: The One Percent. *Journal of Economic Perspectives*, pp. 43-45

Solow, Robert (2014b). Thomas Piketty Is Right. *New Republic* April 22

Sonnenschein, Hugo (1972). Market excess demand functions. *Econometrica* 40:549–563

Sugden, Robert (2002). Credible worlds: the status of theoretical models in economics. In U. Mäki (Ed.), *Fact and fiction in economics* (pp. 107-136). Cambridge: Cambridge University Press

Sugden, Robert (2009). Credible worlds, capacities and mechanisms. *Erkenntnis* 70:3-27

Syll, Lars Pålsson (2001). *Den dystra vetenskapen* ("The dismal science"), Stockholm: Atlas.

Syll, Lars Pålsson (2005). The pitfalls of postmodern economics: remarks on a provocative project. In S. Löfving (ed) *Peopled economies* (pp. 83-114). Uppsala: Interface

Syll, Lars Pålsson (2007a). *Ekonomisk teori och metod: ett kritisk-realistiskt perspektiv* ("Economic theory and method: a critical realist perspective"), 2nd ed, Lund: Studentlitteratur.

Syll, Lars Pålsson (2007b). *John Maynard Keynes*. Stockholm: SNS Förlag

Syll, Lars Pålsson (2011). *Ekonomisk doktrinhistoria* ("History of Economic Thought") Lund: Studentlitteratur

Torsvik, Gaute (2006). *Människonatur och samhällstruktur* ("Human Nature and Social Structure"). Göteborg: Daidalos

Toulmin, Stephen (2003). *The uses of argument*. Cambridge: Cambridge University Press

Varian, Hal (1998). What Use is Economic Theory? In S. Medema & W. Samuels, *Foundations of Research in Economics: How Do Economists Do Economics?* (pp 238-47). Cheltenham: Edward Elgar

Varian, Hal (2006). *Intermediate Microeconomics: A Modern Approach*. (7th ed.) New York: W. W. Norton & Company

Vercelli, Alessandro (1991), *Methodological foundations of macroeconomics: Keynes and Lucas*. Cambridge: Cambridge University Press.

Weintraub, Roy (1979). *Microfoundations: the compatibility of microeconomics and macroeconomics*. Cambridge: Cambridge University Press

On the use and misuse of theories and models in economics

Wong, Stanley (2006). *The foundations of Paul Samuelson's revealed preference theory*. London, Routledge

Zaman, Asad (2012). Methodological Mistakes and Econometric Consequences, *International Econometric Review* 4:99-122

Lightning Source UK Ltd.
Milton Keynes UK
UKOW05f0608220217
295025UK00006B/153/P

9 781848 901841